GARAGE SALE Mania!

Chris Harold Stevenson

How to Hold a Profitable Garage, Yard, or Tag Sale

BETTERWAY PUBLICATIONS, INC.
WHITE HALL, VIRGINIA

Published by Betterway Publications, Inc.
Box 219
Crozet, VA 22932

Cover design by Deborah B. Chappell
Typography by Chappell Graphics

Library of Congress Cataloging in Publication Data

Stevenson, Chris Harold
    Garage sale mania!

    Includes index.
    1. Garage sales. I. Title.
HF5482.3.S74   1988   658.8'7   88-19411
ISBN 1-55870-106-0 (pbk.)

Printed in the United States of America
9 8 7 6 5 4 3 2 1

To my mom, Bunny, my best friend,
and sister Jorlene, Bubby's gal.

ACKNOWLEDGMENTS

I would like to thank the following people:

Art Post, for his never ending enthusiasm, who said that it should be done, and dared me to do it. He is credited with the original concept and many of the ideas herein.

Bryce Littlejohn, for his help with pen and ink.

C. V. Mays and Lee W. Clark, for their wonderful tour through ANTIQUES OF THE WORLD.

Bill Guzzardo, our block sale sponsor, who regularly brings the community together under a common theme.

Don McFarland, of MCFARLAND COMPUTERS, for simplifying the strange and wonderful world of computer technology.

Robyn Gordon of the VALLEY INDOOR SWAP MEET, for sending all of the information with permission to reprint.

Barbara Earnest, a.k.a. Miss B's Secretarial Service, for her exquisite typing and editing abilities.

Dick Fawcett and Erskine Carter, two very special editor/writer friends of mine. They told me that the sky was the limit, when my plane was on the ground.

Finally, my deep appreciation to BETTERWAY PUBLICATIONS, for their professional courtesy and inexplicable faith. They truly have a better way.

CONTENTS

INTRODUCTION

This book has universal and international appeal for age groups ranging from children to adults of any working class, position, or occupation. The theme and content has, indeed, a worldwide flavor. Barring people who live in grass huts and caves, it is common knowledge that a large percentage of persons on this Earth have cellars, attics, garages, carport storage bins, vacant lots, rented storage facilities, and fenced properties. In or on these above mentioned premises are man's accumulations of discarded items: mechanical devices, appliances, recreational equipment, antiques, memorabilia, clothing, keepsakes, and other general neglected flotsam.

Man is, and has been, the proverbial pack rat since the dawn of time, forever clinging dearly to items that he has convinced himself have great sentimental or practical value. But he is sorely reminded of how his possessions continue to multiply and gather dust. His wasteful and materialistic attitude has garnered for him the self-proclaimed ideal, that if it's old and unkempt, it's presently useless.

Ladies and gentlemen, I lead a revival into the not-so-old-and-musty landscapes of our past to discover just what lies beneath the carpet of dust in our cellars, attics, and garages. I'm here to tell you that there's gold in them thar hills! Suddenly, we don't have to travel to that lonely curio shop down the road. We've awakened to a sense of increased practicality, where our best friends are the local merchants and we, ourselves, have prosperous outlets for goods that we can truly say are ours to sell.

We are all natural born trader/sellers and buyers in the great shopping mall of life, where a true bargain is always just a shout away. It's right under our noses. It always has been — waiting for us to allow it a little more dignity. The wave is finally cresting, and people from every walk of life are not afraid to acknowledge the discovery, the fun and innocent exhilaration in, GARAGE SALE MANIA!

Chapter One

THE PSYCHOLOGY OF THE BUYER

Who's Afraid of the Big Bad Wolf?

The increase in the cost of living, according to a recent consumer price index figure for commodities, less food, is approximately 300 percent, or about a 200 percent average rise from a 1967 starting frame to the present. In instances of several items, including durable appliances, the increases have risen even higher, due to consumer demand and competitive foreign markets. These figures bring up a question: Does your income increase enough to keep up with inflation? If you are working for a reputable parent company, the answer might be yes, just barely. Many of us are fortunate to break even in cost versus income statistics. Many of us, however, are not afforded the privilege of working for a company or business that even considers a decent cost of living increase. As a result, we are becoming more cost-conscious. We have become a world of bargain hunters and coupon clippers — deal-hungry mongers, shopping for that ultimate discount. That seems to be our only way of fighting back sometimes — pitting one merchant against another, to eke out the best deal that our pockets can afford. It is our ammunition; our last stand against rising costs and the inflationary scourge.

There is really no such thing as a set price, for we as the consumers often determine the value of commodities by our interest or demand. (Nothing is written in marble.) Fads and trends often have an adverse effect on the stability of a market, many times to our disadvantage. It seems the more we pay attention to a product, the more popular it becomes. And yes, this does bring price wars. But are we really getting that great deal? Or are we caught up in competitive peer pressure? Are we under the illusion that we honestly have taken advantage of that sale because they told us that we did? That brings us to the shopping craze.

Let's admit it, just once, then we can get it out of the way. Doesn't it feel good to walk into a clean, respectable department store where everybody is dressed nicely and suddenly everyone smells sweeter, pull an item from a rack or shelf and plop down a piece of plastic for the purchase? As you stand there before the checker or sales clerk, aren't you momentarily stabbed with a feeling of pride and accomplishment? You are making a statement, aren't you? You're saying, I can afford this store. As a matter of fact, I prefer to shop here and this time, you, (store) had the item that I was looking for. In other words, you're saying that you belong there — you're not out of your element.

There is something egotistical inherent in all of us when it comes to spending money. Have you ever laid down a considerable amount for a purchase and walked away with a feeling that you did them a favor? Perhaps the salesperson would get a nice bonus or a pat on the back because of the purchase you made? Did you actually linger at the counter after the transaction was made, and knowingly expect that thank you? Did you make a friend with the salesperson? Was that, (heaven forbid) salesperson, impressed with your financial prowess? Did you expect just a little admiration back, on the part of the establishment? OF COURSE YOU DID! You are human.

Shopping visits are sometimes the only basic contact we have with strangers, and yes, we do make friends and derive pleasure from the purchase itself. Simply, you gave that person, or store, something of yours and they, in turn, exchanged with you. Tit for tat. And if it was a cash exchange, in large denominations, it was probably made you feel like a miniature industrialist. Maybe even a minor demi-god. Cash nowadays does turn heads. When you left that clean respectable polished (soft music) establishment, didn't you feel just as respectable? We won't talk about how deep in debt you went for the purchase, how many fights you and your spouse were inclined to get into over the incident, or how many sleepless nights you spent lying awake, wondering how you were going to pay off the credit gods. You knew what you were doing, remember? At least most of us have learned not to stretch expenditures beyond our means. We spend sleepless nights convincing ourselves of this fact.

There are alternatives in shopping styles and techniques. Some shopping trips are sheer drudgery, especially when it is a necessity item like an elbow joint for your bathroom sink, the joint looking like a swollen piece of macaroni ready to burst. That is a must item, and must be obtained quickly, or else everybody in the household had best learn how to swim. But for a particular item that you would like to have and are in no rush to buy, like a camera for an upcoming vacation or a typewriter for a special project, can be found and probably at such a reduced rate that your pocket will sigh in relief and thank you tenfold — in cash.

Of course, you are going to have to give up a little ego, soft music, and casual acquaintances at your local department store. You're going to have to step out into the real world and yes, rub shoulders with others like you. You're going to have to learn how to barter, how to say "no," and when to say, "It's a deal." You're going to relearn how to dress yourself in casual and comfortably fitting clothes (which shouldn't be too much of a problem). You'll have to learn how to read a map, if you haven't already. You might have to drop a few superficial airs. You'll learn patience and pace. Most importantly, you are going to learn how to appreciate and become acquainted with real people just like yourself, many of whom will be your neighbors in your own community. And ironically, you'll have to get used to the idea of saving hundreds, possibly thousands of dollars, year after year. Sound like a preachment? Nah, it's going to be just plain fun, and you'll wonder why you hadn't considered it before. How? you ask. Why, garage sales, of course!

Let's talk about the benefits with an example that I can cite off the top of my head. A while back I was considering the purchase of a copy machine, since I do a great deal of short story writing. I was becoming despondent (not to mention broke) in relying on the services of a copying or printing shop. Since I needed thousands of copies, I found that if I continued to pay five cents per page, I would soon be out of a writing career. Oh, I visited the nice showrooms that displayed the latest models and I think I found that I would have to pay in excess of $800.00 for a machine that would stand up to the demands of constant use. My alternative was to search the classified ads, where I stumbled upon a garage sale announcement. The ad offered a used copy machine in the diggings. I called the seller and she informed me that she did have a Sharpfax SF-726 copier for sale. She said that it was big one and she suspected that it was of a commercial variety. This was music to my ears. Commercial, I thought. That meant that it was rugged!

When I arrived at her address to look the machine over, I found that it was not only rugged looking, but quite large and heavy. All the seller said was that it had worked some time ago in a now defunct business. We plugged it in (at my request) and it did cycle. However, it would need a few products before it was shipshape (primarily, a package of photosensitive masters, which don't keep when a copier sits for any length of time). So I took a gamble, paid $125.00 for it, got my receipt, and lugged the machine home. I spent $75.00 on the copy machine for a P.M. kit (preventive maintenance), which included a bunny brush, developer, toner, and photosensitive masters. I put it to work the very next day (thanks due to the generous repair

A used copy machine for
$125.00

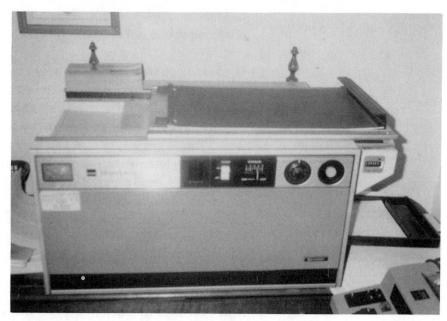

technician who gave of his time and advice on instructions and operation).

To this day, I have logged 8000 perfect copies on this machine, and my total savings, less paper costs, have amounted to over $350.00: this, provided I would have used one of the popular copy services. In another three months this purchase will have nearly paid for itself three times over! Though I did not receive a warranty with this item for obvious reasons, I did manage to secure an owner's manual that has instructed me on how to perform all manner of light repairs and maintenance. Copy machine technicians require $75.00 per hour just to step into your home and stare deeply — this is excluding extra parts.

I'm reminded of another time when I wanted to add a second typewriter to use as a backup in case my present model decided to go on strike. I found a neat little IBM model C machine at the local swap meet, and for $15.00 had myself another machine. Cleaning the plastic kick cams and the power roller on this model, I set it to working just fine. I've since used it to write several scripts.

Both of these examples mentioned were lucky breaks. A little knowledge helped out as well. But not all merchandise purchased from garage sales and swap meets is functional. Appearances can be deceiving. Some items are obviously known to be past the point of repair (known sometimes only to the present owner) and these items are, or can be, doctored up in an attempt to off the dead product. It could be anything wrong with the item from an obscure customized bolt that was impossible to find, to a major component without which the item would be useless. It takes a basic but good general mechanical knowledge and a keen eye to discover what is a bargain and what's not. I have a small encyclopedia of fix-it books that I refer to occasionally. These sources help me determine beforehand the worst possible scenario that could present itself if I happened to buy a questionable item. I've also researched the parent companies and their brand names; forever on the lookout for items or products that have been discontinued, shunned, or reclaimed by the manufacturers. Also a little investigation into the history of an item might reveal the reason for its dysfunction.

Once, I discovered that the reason for the malfunction of an electronic game was because its batteries were reversed in the carriage. It was terribly simple to effect a cure. Since then, I have learned to inspect the position of batteries in all devices that use them. I carry new spare batteries (of different sizes) in my car when I need to look for a battery-operated appliance.

I bought a G. E. room fan at a garage sale once, and the seller assured me that the motor was burned out. I noticed that the electrical cord was gray and smooth near the plug position, which indicated that the cord had been yanked from the socket many times (improper disconnecting procedure) and on a hunch, I bought the fan and took it home. There, I repaired it by splicing into the undamaged section of wire and attaching a new universal plug. For a burned out motor, it's surprising how that fan cools things down now.

My brother-in-law (who can run down an electrical short until it's out of breath) helped me with one of my neighbor's appliances once. He diagnosed a problem in an electrically heated clothes dryer. The owner of the dryer was distraught and ready to call the junk man (I hate that word) but we found the problem to be a shorted out strip-heater. Twenty-one dollars and one hour later, the machine was functioning again, much to the shock and bewilderment of the owner. Typically, the purchase of a used dryer would have amounted to at least $150.00 had the original dryer not been repaired.

Not everyone is a handyman or mechanically inclined. But some logical and deductive reasoning is in order when purchasing used items, (motorized) things that go wing, zing, whir or bzzzzzz...or are supposed to, at any rate. It doesn't take a genius to know that a camera with a broken shutter mechanism is useless until you consider the fact that it can be repaired (if the quality of the camera warrants it) and at considerably less expense than the cost of a new storebought model. Beginning to get the picture?

NEGOTIATING PRICES

Shopping garage sales and swap meets offers a unique flexibility in the bottom-line cost of merchandise. If items are not plainly marked at these events, there is reason to assume that you can, and will, have a say in the determination of a final purchase price. You have a voice. Stand up and be recognized. No one will ever bite your head off for asking a seller for a reduced price on any item. In fact, the seller might even delight in some light and honest bickering. (In some Middle Eastern countries it is regarded as an insult to buy spontaneously without haggling over the cost.) If you feel that an item is priced beyond its reasonable value, explain this to the seller along with your reasons for thinking so. Any technical expertise that you can relay about the knowledge of an item can only help you in reasoning with the seller, then arriving at some compromise that is beneficial to both of you. If you are extremely well versed in the knowledge of a product — don't show off. You're apt to bore or irritate the seller and, lose a deal. Be reasonable and precise in your motives and expectations. You will find that most people are willing to deal with a pleasant personality, rather than with a loudmouth who insists that the seller is a crook who doesn't know what he's talking about.

ETIQUETTE

Garage sales are not free-for-alls. No matter what condition you find items in at a sale, be reminded that they are private property and hold at least some significance and value to the owner. Ask to see or touch things first. Don't blatantly handle objects or attempt to dismantle them without permission. There might be others waiting to see the same item. It is unwise and discourteous to tie up a seller with your persistent need to dismantle his product piece by piece in front of him, while the seller has other pressing needs at the moment like conducting his sale and keeping track of inventory and transactions.

Above all, have confidence in your ability to wager. Know that deals are aplenty — happening every day. Sales are numerous and the opportunity for finding that ultra-bargain is always just around the corner. And in garage sales, everyone is a winner.

Chapter Two

GARAGE SALES — WHAT ARE THEY?

A Basket Full of Goodies

What's in a name? Actually, the term garage sale is misleading since it would be inappropriate to put part of your house up for sale. Rather, the term implies items and possessions that have been stockpiled in a garage or carport, that are at some point in time offered for sale, usually on a weekend day (Saturday or Sunday), during daylight hours. Such items would include, for example: boxed books, garden and automotive tools, tires and rims, furniture, sports equipment, used appliances, clothes, and just about any other item that a family has deemed discards or junk (there's that word again!).

The "garage" can be the attic or cellar of a house that doesn't have a garage. It is the overflow point for extra stuff that we don't want in our household for

Typical garage sale

some reason or another. The garage is often cluttered with things that just get in our way (this seems to be the American way, in particular). Although I have seen some garages that are as neat and spiffy as some kitchens. Most of the time, though, the reverse is true, since we are dealing with the average family here. The garage can really be a jungle out there. I am reminded of one customer at a local garage sale who happened to open a box that was for sale. Inside, he found stacks of old classic record albums...along with a dozen newborn rats. The potential buyer asked the seller a pertinent question: "Do the rats come along with the deal?" The seller, without missing a beat, improvised quickly, "Animal life is one dollar apiece!"

When a house or apartment is filled to the rafters, the reasonable overflow point is certain to be the garage, where often space is found in plenty: on shelves, racks, on the floor, under benches, and in the rafters. Then the time comes when the occupants find it difficult to move around the clutter, or find anything that is worth looking for (never mind about the car, it was excommunicated from its rightful lodging years ago). Hence, the family arrives at the decision to exhibit and sell these family relics, heirlooms, and mechanical misfits. The family spends Friday night (possibly Thursday) sorting through the debris looking for interesting objects of merit and value. It is usually at this time that family members transform instantly into archaeologists or historians. For the first time in neighborhood history, heated discussion and raised voices emanate from the Jones' house, and phrases like: "You're not selling that!" and "How could you? I had that when I was a baby," break the pall of silence on that Friday night. Everybody becomes an expert on what should go and what should stay.

Some family members are likely to cause a deliberate distraction, then sneak off to their room with a Donald Duck night light palmed in their hand, then repeat the process over again, bringing the stuff right back into the house.

You'd think that some people were performing last rites over their possessions before they were designated for sale. It is a time for sentiment and the remembrance of things old and dear. It is a time to gather your treasures, for you may never have another chance to reclaim those cherished but useless belongings. Some people have great difficulty in severing these types of bonds. On the brighter side, they could think of it as a revelation, in that it will probably be the first time they have ever seen the garage clean and organized. So with the sacrifice comes a little solace, after all.

*Garage sale with some
grounded items*

YARD SALES

A yard sale is a garage sale that's gotten too big for its britches. There isn't enough room on the driveway so extra merchandise is shifted to the lawn space. Articles in a yard sale are usually displayed on tarps or blankets. Or the occupant of the sale house wishes to use the driveway, so the standard command is: "Keep it on the grass." Of course some folks like to use the yard as a display area, especially in the summer months when the climate is warmer; the lounge chair is a more relaxed vantage point, the lemonade flows like a small river, and the tanning lotion gets uncorked. A yard sale doubles as a cut-rate campout.

MOVING SALES

Now I wish that I could use this title every time I had a garage sale. These people and their robust displays really clean up: large items such as heavy appliances and furniture, small motorized vehicles, collapsible pools, bedding and clothes, and other quality pieces — the elite of any buyer's dreams, are to be found at these sales. There's a hint of desperation associated with the words, "moving sale" usually followed by the stipulation, "everything must go." Since moving sales are usually more thought out and planned, the presentation of goods is sometimes more organized and appealing. This type of sale often includes an open invitation to potential buyers to enter the home where select furniture is left in the rooms, this being a good marketing technique since buyers can gauge the relative sizes and dimensions of furniture sets and groupings. Not to mention, of course, the sellers' reluctance to move such heavy pieces out onto their lawns and driveways, knowing that if they fail to sell them, they have to be ushered back into the premises at the expense of several back muscles. But not to mention this, of course.

Since moving sales are usually more thought out and planned, the presentation of items is often better. A moving sale combined with a garage sale is truly a treasure trove. It's evident that these sellers are motivated in acquiring enough money to assist them in relocating (minus some extra burdens like real nice furniture).

Some of the best buys on large items and appliances are found at the moving sales, and if you find a piece that you feel is marked too high, you can always bid on it, then reconnect with the seller (before he moves) to find out if your bid has won out.

I would not put any money down as a retainer to hold an item. Not in a moving sale. You might find yourself busy with other responsibilities and after finally remembering that you left a deposit on a promised piece of furniture at a moving sale, you arrive upon the seller's doorstep to find that he has indeed moved, with your deposit.

There is another variety of moving sale where the seller never moves or is not planning to pack up. A bit sneaky perhaps, but a tactic sometimes used to assist in the urgency of a sale. This also applies to "death in the family," "divorce," or "won in game show" notices. A telltale sign that it is not a legitimate moving sale would be evidence of extremely high or abnormal prices on goods. A legitimate mover would be more prone (on the average) to keep sale items at a reasonable amount for quick release. Secondly, if you see that the no-good-nik is still at his residence after a year's time, this would be a clear-cut indication. The ethics of the question are not the important thing. The important thing is for you to find a legitimate and affordable price (and I have only seen this practice used twice in five years).

SWAP MEETS

We call them swap meets and flea markets; neither term is indicative of the event. Nobody swaps items (rarely, unless it is advertised as such) at swap meets, but rather pays for purchases with cash and sometimes a check. No one sells fleas at a flea market; it's another name for a swap meet, which can include the large county varieties, as well.

Swap meets are a delight in that they attract numerous talented craftspeople and artists who carry and exhibit some very unusual handcrafted and original items. You can find works of art (paintings), sculpture, textiles, jewelry, and most other artsy fare at these gatherings. In addition, you'll find goods typical of regular store bought merchandise. You'll find shade, maybe a place to sit down, and refreshments at most large swap meets. Many schools, drive-in theaters, colleges, and corporations with large parking lots sponsor weekly or monthly events. Some meets have contest drawings; some charge admission, and some don't. Standard admission prices might set you back a couple of bucks but it's worth the price to experience a garage sale on a grand scale.

College held swap meet

Why the common items at a swap meet are slightly higher than at neighborhood garage sales has always been a mystery to me. Might it be a hint of that prestige factor that we associate with walking into that department store? Since swap meets are definitely larger in scale and require a selling permit, maybe we can just chalk it up to what we could call a quantity tax, and let it go at that.

More about this later in the selling section, but briefly: to set up, display, and sell items at a swap meet, you'll need an area or booth. You can acquire these by phoning the sponsor of the meet in advance and for a fee for the day or two's privilege of displaying your goods, you can set up your small shop and expect to do quite well. The area or booth costs range in price from ten to fifty dollars (and up) for a spot per day. Not bad, considering that you could recoup those investments in the first two or three hours after opening.

A word of caution on swap meets: they are prone to attract individuals who are likely to carry, yes, some stolen articles. It has happened, and there have been increasing crackdowns on this type of behavior. This practice of trying to fence or sell stolen goods is what has given swap meets and flea markets (even garage sales) a bad name. It ruins it for serious sellers and buyers alike. Pay particular attention to car stereos, hubcaps and wheels, home entertainment units, and such items that are most commonly stolen from the public. Beware of any serial numbers that have been altered or obliterated from any items, for this is an indication that the item cannot now or ever be traced to its original owner.

Finally, swap meets and flea markets are notorious for items that are clones, fakes, replicas, or imitations. There has been an endless glut of Levi jean imitators, as well as copies of other high quality, brand name clothing. For you men, I trust you can tell the difference between genuine Snap On or Craftsman tools and their lesser known counterparts; usually given regal names of status, such as Eagle, Master Work, Goliath, or some such similar fabricated brand name. Just because it's triple chrome plated doesn't make it a durable investment.

Vendor setup at swap meet

As for computer hardware, I've seen it go from the boss pack drive, to the eight inch floppy, to the five and a quarter, to the three and a half inch sizes. Now the new kid on the block is the 32 bit microprocessor. It's user friendly this, compatible that, and clone wars all over again. Exercise extreme caution when purchasing these items at swap meets. Where computers, VCRs, stereos, and other similar equipment are concerned, you should thoroughly research your specific product needs before attempting to make such large investments. I would not recommend buying these items from a swap meet unless the merchant was a bona fide representative of the brand name affixed to his products. And for such items, I would insist that they be new, demonstrated to my satisfaction, and that they accompany an instruction packet with a warranty enclosed.

BLOCK SALES

These events are usually sponsored by individuals or agencies and they are nothing more than garage sales on a mass scale, situated in a group of homes or a housing tract. The convenience here is that you don't have to drive long distances to visit many sale sites at once. They are all grouped together in one neighborhood. The quantity and variety of items to be found is endless. You're sure to find something interesting at these affairs. Prices are extremely good and the competition among the sellers is fierce. These events win the public over with sheer hospitality and an open friendliness amongst the shoppers that is hard to top anywhere. Everybody seems to run into each other at block sales, frequently making various stops and chatting to acquaintances that they have seen at other sales. At well organized block sales, flyers are often provided by the sponsors. On these flyers are small advertisements, but more importantly, maps to direct the consumer to the various sale houses. Sometimes they contain an items list in which the addresses have the particular merchandise that buyers are looking for. These sales have to top the list for bargains and just plain friendly people.

OPEN HOUSES

On the East Coast of the United States, the term open house often designates the intention of a garage sale. On the East Coast garage sales are also often called yard or lawn sales. Typically, on the West Coast the term open house is an invitation associated with the actual sale of a house and its property. A West Coast open house is advertised by realtors and it denotes that the owners of the house wish to show the interior and property to prospective buyers before a purchase is made.

MISCELLANEOUS

Other notable sale events of interest to the consumer that offer reduced rates are: police auctions, estate sales, rummage sales, business liquidations, and department store sidewalk or parking lot sales. Consult your local newspaper for information on the times and locations of these special events.

DRIVING AND SAFETY

A word about travel and locating garage sales and block sales: always use extreme care when searching for the address of a sale. Refer to a map beforehand. Garage sale signs are sometimes obscure and poorly rendered. They are tacked to trees, telephone poles, and taped on walls. Sometimes you would think that the signs were made by clumsy six year olds, and sometimes this is the case. You'll find yourself squinting, trying to follow that little maze of faded arrows that point every which way but to the right direction or address.

Have a passenger concentrate on deciphering the signs and the directions to the sale house so that the driver can attend to the driving. Park in authorized areas. Don't leave your car double parked or running. Be mindful of children, especially when attending block sales. The small ones abound at these events and the excitement runs high. Children are liable to exit a vehicle quickly and dash across a street in pursuit of a stuffed teddy. Don't gamble — play it safe and drive the speed limit. Most speed limits in housing tracts are twenty-five miles per hour or less. In school zones they are sometimes fifteen miles per hour.

Chapter Three

WHAT ARE YOU LOOKING FOR
A Tisket, A Tasket

You're going to have to be reasonable in what you expect to find at a typical garage sale. (We will confine ourselves to garage sale shopping, for simplicity.) If you are in the market for a specialty item, like a La Marque ladies analog quartz watch, you would be advised to check your local classified newspaper or magazine, where such an item would fall under the category of Jewelry. The chances are good that you can locate (nearly) the item that you are searching for in these publications. Since these items are listed individually, you can expect to pay more as this is a concentrated effort by the seller to advertise this specialty piece. In our community, for example, the names of the publications that have this type of information are: *The Recycler, The Penny Saver,* the *Nifty Nickel,* and *The Super Saver.* Also, the large city and county newspapers have sections devoted to the sale of merchandise.

Let's confine ourselves to some basic and popular items commonly found at garage sales. It's a sure bet that with a few inquiries you will be able to locate the following: antique furniture, aquariums, art and decorator items, baby accessories, bathroom and plumbing supplies, household furniture, beds and mattresses, bikes, books, calculators, cameras, camping quipment, clocks, clothing, computer systems, dryers and washers, exercise equipment, freezers, musical instruments, housewares, luggage, stoves, electric motors, office supplies, optical equipment, paintings, radios, gardening supplies, records, refrigerators, rugs, sewing machines, silverware, sporting goods, stereos, tape recorders, telephones, tools (hand and power), typewriters, vacuum cleaners, and home video units

It's never to your disadvantage to call up sellers before a sale and request that an item be put on hold until you arrive and inspect it for possible purchase. Just make sure that you arrive early and make your decision. This will free the time up for the rest of the sale in case you reject it. You might, at that time, ask for approximate prices of items, and with further calls to other sales, be able to make a comparison. A little phone work can keep your travel expenses down.

You can always ask what a seller's exchange or return policy is. A return policy or money back guarantee is uncommon in garage sale purchasing, although I have run across several sellers who will promise some type of small guarantee. It never hurts to ask. This policy is a rarity since most items sold in this fashion are assumed as is purchases. The as is designation means that the item or goods is sold in its present condition — whether that state is functional or not. In other words, the owner has stated that he is not responsible for merchandise after a purchase, and once you've made the transaction, it's your baby. Receipts that include this phrase will hold up in court of law to protect the interest of the seller. It's kind of a belated I told you so. As is terminology is frequently applied to used automobile contracts, which void any guarantee or warranty.

Regarding money back agreements: it never hurts to ask. Many sellers will cooperate with a buyer to garner repeat business. These sellers usually hold regular and frequent sales. It is to their advantage to show some type of flexibility, especially when buyers live in close proximity.

HOW MUCH WILL IT COST?

How much will it cost? This question covers a very wide and gray (unknown) area. Kelly has his *Blue Book* to list the comparative prices of used automobiles. R. S. Yeoman has his *Guide Book of United States Coins*, commonly referred to as the Red Book. We'll have to approximate our own guidelines for used goods.

Having participated in many garage sales, both as a buyer and seller, I have arrived at a basic rule of thumb which states: you can reasonably expect to save fifty to seventy percent on most items, on the average. The super deals, which are not rare, can save you as much as ninety percent of the original retail cost, and this is allowing the fact, of course, that the item might be anywhere from six months to thirty years old, or much older. The dates of manufacture play an important part in your selection and decision making. Obviously, the newer the item, the more relaxed you can feel about its operability. Also, parts availability is better with newer items.

Antiques can break the rule of thumb that older is not better, or older should be cheaper. Coins, dolls, stamps, vintage wine, weapons, furniture, crafted artifacts, memorabilia, and other such collectibles can be expected to cost many times their original retail value. In pursuit of collector's items the buyer should be very familiar with the merchandise that he intends to purchase. It would be helpful, for example, for anyone searching for vintage military firearms to invest in a copy of Paul Wahl's *Gun Traders Guide* or a similar text. Jewelry might well be included in this category, and any good reference manual or guidebook on the subject would help to distinguish present day value and what you would expect to pay for it secondhand. In looking for collectibles (comic books, baseball cards, old bottles, etc.) research is a must. All popular collector's items have publications — some of which are membership oriented. These references are precise and reliable sources — many of them are constantly updated.

I would not take anyone's word on the value of an item, since their true knowledge on the subject might be in question. Or there might be a tendency to exaggerate or misrepresent, even though the seller could be sincere in his/her intentions. You are responsible for your own footwork and research. To protect yourself, I urge you to purchase these sources and read them frequently, including the updated editions, to gain some expertise on the subject material. It's a good habit and well worth the cost of a guidebook or manual.

Some examples of guidebooks for items include:

Antique Monthly, Boone Inc.

Price Guide To Antique And Classic Cameras, Centennial Publications

Bicycle Seller, (local edition)

Computer Buyers Guide, Signet

Gun Traders Guide, Stoeger

Guide Book of United States Coins, Western Publishing Company

Collector's World, Collector's World Publishing

Tobacco Tins, Old Bottle Collecting Publications

Collector Editions, Collector Communications Corp.

Dollspart, Dollspart Supply Co.

American Book Collector, American Books Collector Publications

American Clay Exchange, Page One Publishing

Dolls, The Collectors Magazine, Collectors Communication Corp.

National Knife Magazine, (Official Journal of the National Knife Collector Association)

Scott Stamp Monthly, Scott Stamp Publications

Tri State Trader, Mayhill Publishing

PAYING FOR PURCHASES

Work with cash. If you have found an item that you like, pay for it in cash, up front. Paying for items with a check is risky business, and it's the seller who bears the brunt of disappointment when he suddenly finds himself the recipient of numerous personal checks that wouldn't pay the cost of their own printing (due to insufficient bank funds). Garage sales are of a personal nature and it's best to work with cash in these instances. If the seller happens to be a neighbor a check might be all right, provided he agrees to this method of payment. If you absolutely must pay for an item with a check, provide the seller with your current driver's license number, address, phone number, and other pertinent information. You might, as a courtesy, bring along a recent bank balance statement to indicate that you do have sufficient funds to cover the cost of merchandise.

Forget about credit cards at these events. No one has the time or facilities to contact a local credit service to verify your creditworthiness. The only exception in credit card purchasing would be at one of the larger county swap meets, where the vendors are prepared for such transactions. Large auctions, where bidding is commonplace, are also known to accept checks and credit card purchasing.

Chapter Four

APPROACHING A SALE

Over the River and Through the Woods

Now that you have an idea of what you are looking for, you're ready to go. You might make your trip to a garage sale a family outing. It's great for the kids since they often meet other children there who are perhaps, involved in the sale itself. It's rather comical to watch children play grown up and bid with other children for choice toys. Their approach is always uncomplicated and direct. Phrases like "Give me the money" or "I want that" leave little doubt as to their intentions. We as adults can learn a great deal by watching the smaller folks. I've seen children shake on a deal in sixty seconds time, and the deal wouldn't have been any better if prolonged.

BEST TIMES AND DAYS

You can search out and find a garage sale any day of the week. The more common days for sales will be in the spring and summer months. The best selling days are Friday, Saturday, and Sunday.

Friday is not a popular day for a sale, but it is used more than any other weekday. I always thought that the sellers who sold on Friday did so because they associated that day with a paycheck. It's true, the majority of the working class are paid on Fridays. However, that same majority are still on the job up until quitting time. That can be anywhere from 4:00 to 7:00 P.M.

If a working consumer is interested in a Friday sale they should get to the sale quickly. The sun has a nasty habit of going down. That must be the reason why I have seen floodlights used in a Friday evening/night sale.

Friday is also less popular because it is a last working day. Many people make plans for outings on the weekends, and Friday is the day of preparation. Hence, Friday afternoons and evenings are a little rushed for everyone. The traffic always seems heavier and the frantic dash to get home prevails.

Saturday is the prime day of any garage sale. The majority of us are off on the weekends. We have Saturday to do virtually anything we want, knowing that we have a day of recuperation, Sunday, ahead of us. The chances of finding a one-day Saturday sale, or a two-day weekend sale, are excellent.

You will find the heaviest activity on Saturday, both with the buyers and sellers. Expect to go as early as possible. We're talking about the crack of dawn, around 7:00 A.M. Why so early? The best deals are to be had then. Everyone knows that the first on the scene is sure to get the best bargains. The first on the scene has his choice of as much as he wants, and whatever he wants. The bulk of any Saturday garage sale will be sold out between the hours of 7:00 A.M. and 11:00 A.M. The magic hours seem to be 8:00 A.M. to 10:00 A.M. A further breakdown reveals the hours between 8:30 and 9:30 to be the heaviest time of trading. Any seller worth his salt will be awake and set up by 7:00 A.M. He knows that you are coming. He has to be prepared.

Sunday is typically a day of rest. Many people attend church on Sunday. The crowds at the swap meets and garage sales are noticeably thinner, by as much as forty percent. Many of the best deals were made on Saturday (if it has been a two-day sale). So on Sunday, things are toning down, with sporadic sales throughout the day.

The early morning Sunday sale can still be a great find. Since a seller might have run Saturday, he is certain to have restocked with a few more goods for the Sunday sale, particularly if he has done well. And if he has, this will give him the incentive to try on Sunday. Follow the Saturday sale time guides for Sunday as well.

BEFORE THE PURCHASE — DEMONSTRATIONS

Once at a sale, you will find yourself shoulder to shoulder with other curious people who have the same idea that you have. What neat thing can I pick up for almost nothing? Let's face it: we all have visions of finding lost treasure. There is something adventurous in our spirit that demands that we go on that epic quest now and then.

Be keen in your observations of other buyers around you. There are professionals out there. Professional treasure hunters. They have precise motives, ruthless hearts, and a lot of money. They actually make their living shopping garage sales. Their incomes are not as skimpy as you might think, either. Collectibles have been the biggest reason for the appearance of the professionals, with antiques leading the pack for the most sought after treasures.

One day, I watched a professional in action. He had arrived early, like me, at a local garage sale. I watched him rummage through a stack of old furniture, until he found a piece that caught his interest — an old bureau desk with a cracked oval mirror. He went through the drawers, pulling them in and out, reaching in and around the joints of the legs and frame. He did not smile. He did not frown. He showed little or no emotion, and one could say that he truly had a poker face. My vision was obscured at some times, and I did not see everything that he did in examining the desk. After he had made his inspection, he got into a polite haggling match with the seller. At the end of the deal, the professional got his desk for $20.00.

As he was loading the desk onto his flatbed truck (full of other victory prizes) I asked him, "How did you know?" Why that piece? What was so urgent about it?

He replied, tight-lipped, "I knew that it was circa 1800 but I wanted to be sure. It was the old letter wedged in the frame that confirmed it. It was dated 1865, August. Not a real good deal, but better than most."

He assured me that it was a lucky break to find a dated letter in the old desk, but it had happened before so he was always sure to check the cracks and crevices for telltale evidence. Before I could question him further, he was in the cab of his truck, reading his next garage sale address (his battle map), and before I could blink he was racing off down the street — another adventure calling out to him.

When considering merchandise for sale, ask the seller for a demonstration. In the previous example we saw that the professional buyer was not concerned about permission. When he handled the desk, he was intent on doing things his way. I would not advise that you follow this person's example. He could have easily broken something or scratched the piece. It doesn't take much, just carelessness.

Many times, you will need to check the operability of a motorized appliance or a piece of hardware that has moving parts. Ask the seller if you may look at something before you handle it. For motorized appliances, ask if they may be plugged in.

In most cases I bring an extension cord with me to garage sales. This assures me that if the seller doesn't have a cord, I will have one on hand. I also bring fresh batteries in my glove compartment: 9 volt batteries, and A, C, and D sizes. There's nothing more frustrating than finding an appliance you like and having no way of knowing if it operates.

Most small motors have shafts of some type that revolve and provide momentum. And most of these shafts, or spindles, are carried by bearings. The bearings can be simple pilot holes, or they can be loaded carriers that contain ball or needle type bearings. In small appliances, these bearings are often pre-lubed at the factories, and there is no way to re-lubricate them. A very common malfunction of a small appliance will be in the bearing areas of the motor. Normally, a smoothly running electrical motor will emit a steady hum, and the moving parts of the appliance will function from the energy provided by the motor. If you should hear a metallic grating when any motor isturned on, chances are that a bearing surface is worn or misaligned. If you should detect a foul burning odor and see evidence of smoke, it is a sure bet that the wiring in the motor is shorted, or that the armature is bad. Unless you are an electrician (or know of one), your chances of repairing the device are not good. I would not purchase any appliance that showed these symptoms.

There is another type of malfunction in small motors in which, when plugged in, they do not operate at all. The motor seems frozen. This is not always the case. After the electrical cord has been plugged into an outlet, try gently wiggling the wire at the plug base. Up and down movements work the best. If at this time the motor runs, then cuts out every time you move the wire, it is certain that the electrical cord itself is damaged. A simple cure would be to splice into the damaged wire (away from the plug to an undamaged section of wire), and attach a new universal plug fixture. This is very common in hair dryers, in which the constant movement of the cord causes a break in the wires, usually near the plug position, or where the cord enters the appliance.

Be sure to try out fresh batteries in toys and small appliances that take them. Install the batteries in the proper order when fitting them into the carriages. Note the position and direction of the arrows that indicate the proper battery direction. Check the small wires attached to the leads or pickups. If after these steps the device does not operate, the damage is internal and probably not worth the effort or expense to repair. Small battery-operated toys and such do not have durable electric motors. They are not designed to last for years. It is easier to buy a new electronic game than it is to repair one.

With small gasoline engines, such as the types that are used on lawn mowers, leaf blowers, edgers, trimmers, and chain saws, bearing noises also indicate worn parts. The remedy for an engine that does not start at all could be a tune up. Contact points and condensers frequently burn out, thus breaking the field of electric ignition (the element required to burn fuel). An engine without fuel will not run, nor will it run with contaminated fuel. The engine requires air through the air cleaning device. If the air cleaner is clogged or obstructed, the amount of oxygen present is not sufficient to mix with the fuel, hampering combustion. Therefore, check for the presence of fuel, make sure there are no restrictions in the air cleaning element and that a sufficient amount of spark is reaching the firing plug.

With an engine that runs smoothly and has no symptoms of worn parts or bearing noises, it is recommended that the condition of the exhaust be examined. A clear exhaust indicates a normal running engine. An excessive emission of blue/white smoke would indicate excessive oil consumption: worn piston rings, valve guides, or a blown head gasket. Clouds of black smoke would surely indicate excessive fuel consumption: problems with the carburetor or fuel system. Note that some of the two cycle engines that are used on chain saws and leaf blowers require a mix of oil in direct ratio to the amount of gasoline used. These engines will typically emit moderate amounts of blue/white smoke, since the gasoline contains some oil.

In purchasing TV sets, (color or black and white) ask for a demonstration with the set fully warmed up. Observe the clarity and steadiness of the picture received and watch out for distortion, particularly at the edges of the screen. Listen carefully to the sound reception. The audio ought to be at least as good as your radio's, not only for enjoyment, but because that is another clue to the quality of the entire set.

Remember that portable TVs offer potential repair savings over the larger floor consoles because they can be taken into a repair shop by the customer. TV technicians require an arm and a leg to make a routine service call, especially on the color models.

Note the shades of the image. A poor set will have good contrast of black and white, but will not adjust to get softness in between, or the detail provided by a good set. A poor set has a grainy effect.

Accessibility to the control knobs is another consideration. In the front of the cabinet they are easier to reach, and if they are knob or dial type it is a simple matter to find out if they work, producing the different modes i.e., contrast, vertical and horizontal hold, tone, tint, and brightness.

Some of the better quality color sets include Zenith (models 4030, 3028), Motorola, and RCA. The private brands of some of the major retail chains are also good bargains.

In considering stereo equipment, the component systems offer the most flexibility in adding units to the system (to update), while the separate components themselves, the turntable, equalizer, cassette recorder, etc. are more easily transported for repair purposes. Stereo units, of course, mean a system that uses two or more speakers with sound separation in between. Good low range and high range tonal quality is evidence of a good unit, with little or no distortion on target channels. The power of the stereo unit is typically rated in watts, and they range anywhere from ten watts up to 100 watts and beyond. A good mid-sized model will produce fifty watts per channel, and this is quite adequate for a normal home. Almost every unit sold nowadays has AM and FM capabilities, so consider this feature as a plus.

RCA and Magnavox are prime, quality candidates, along with Pioneer and Panasonic. Again, the major retail department stores and specialty electronic outlets like Radio Shack carry their own quality brand names.

On occasion you will come across computer hardware and video games. With computers you will have to be very careful in considering them for purchase. If you find an IBM compatible computer, Apple, or other major brand name computer, ask the seller to demonstrate the system. Observe if all of the keys register an image on the monitor. If there is not an image on the screen while depressing a certain keyboard character, chances are that the key contact under the plastic key top is dirty. This is not much of a problem. A little alcohol and a cotton swab will clean the connection. If the monitor (screen) remains blank when the computer and monitor are turned on, there might be bad or loose connections in the interface (wire connections). If error messages occur on the screen, it means that you will need the owner's manual to diagnose these problems. If the computer will not turn on at all, check the reset button and any fuse that might be located on the back panel. Again, use great care when purchasing computers. You might take along with you a person who is familiar with computer hardware and software. This person could be of great assistance in helping you to make the best decision. Finally, if you do make a purchase, insist on an up-to-date operations manual for the model that you buy. Without it, you will not be able to realize the potential of the computer or gain access to the many programs that it can perform.

Some of the common video arcade games like Atari and Intellevision are great buys and lots of fun for the family. The older Atari and Intellevision games are still popular, even though some newer brand name competitors have burst on the scene. The old and reliable Pong game is still around, and it is a great bargain secondhand. There is not much that can go wrong with a video game — either it works or it doesn't. Their quality of workmanship is not of the highest standard compared to that of computers.

For demonstration purposes, video arcade games can be hooked up to an appropriate monitor, or they can be attached to the jacks on the back of a regular television set. Be mindful of obtaining the instruction packet with video games, the same as you would with a computer purchase.

With other items that have workable parts you will just have to use some basic common sense. For example, cameras that are not the instamatic type are difficult products in which to determine workability. You can look through the view finder and push the shutter button to see if the mechanism works. Checking the battery compartment for corrosion would also follow in this routine. And that's about all you can do.

If you are looking for a special item, you might spend a little time researching it, with a source or guidebook. Even a quick call to a shop owner or expert can help you determine some basic rules concerning products and how they are supposed to operate.

HAGGLING FOR PROFIT AND FUN

The true test of steel is in its temper. So will it be with your ability to wager for profit. Haggling for profit can be fun. Let's start at the beginning with some basic ground rules.

If you are as smart as you think you are, you will wear old jeans and a T-shirt to garage or estate sales. Shopping these sales does not require formal attire i.e., dresses, suits and ties, sportcoats. Remember, you're just one of the crowd. Arriving and remaining inconspicuous is to your advantage. You don't want to stand out in this crowd. Anything that even hints of a financial position should be discouraged. You wouldn't want to pay more for something just because you looked like you could. So, ladies, leave those mink wraps at home.

If your only car happens to be a new model Cadillac or Mercedes Benz, park the car some distance from the sale. A car is often considered a prestige symbol. Many first impressions are made by the automobile that you own. A seller is always observant of who steps out of what, in his neighborhood. The seller will certainly notice a couple exiting a lavish car near his sale. He then might decide to raise his prices slightly.

If items are not plainly marked at a garage sale (or swap meet sale), chances are the seller will be waiting for you to ask him that all important question, "How much do you want for it?" Begin this way: pick up an item, inquire as to its price, then set it down. Continue the procedure with other goods as though you are browsing, or in a state of wishful thinking. This simple approach sends the seller a signal that you might have little money to spend.

This can work to the buyer's advantage. After the seller has watched you canvas his entire inventory (he sees that faraway look in your eyes), he is likely to take pity on you at some point, and inquire as to your favorite picks. At this point, you can set the hook deeper into his sympathetic soul and explain breathlessly, "There are just so many wonderful things, I don't think that I can afford any of it." If the seller has a doorknob instead of a heart, he won't budge, or be affected by the remark. Fortunately, most of us have soft spots for the weak or penniless, and give in. He should give in. So it's a good bet that he will take an interest in you, especially after you have flattered him with your wonderful things remark. His decision to give you a break might come as, "Well, whatever your little heart desires." This is the "poor me, wonderful you" technique. It has been used on me with devastating success. I'm a sucker for it every time.

There will be times when your opponent is stronger, a seller who knows his worth and feels that he cannot budge for anyone. You will find these types at the larger, regularly held swap meets. These people sell every weekend. The effort is not to supplement their incomes. It is their life. They've heard it all before. They are the professional sellers. Their merchandise will be marked in most cases. They know what they can get because they play the waiting game. For every ten visits to their booth, they know that at least two will buy without question. So they wait it out.

These sellers have a rap (knowledge of their subject and inventory) that is so well tuned, you will believe that they have rehearsed their lines over and over again — shades of an old wild west medicine show! Their expressions will be grim-sober. They will allow little emotion to play on their faces. After all, they've been waiting for you. Is there an offense against this seemingly bulletproof defense? Maybe. Because there is power in knowledge.

The only way that you will get this kind of seller to give you the slightest recognition and/or deal, is to know his subject better than he does. It is your only hope. He will not believe the "wonderful things" line. He's heard it before. So what do you do? You come into his enemy camp just as grim-faced and sober as he is, with a brain filled with facts, figures, and determination. You will not show off or brag, but you will hold your ground with the conviction that you know what you are talking about. Sooner or later, into the discussions, he will show signs of weakening. He might even be impressed with *your* rap.

I can cite an example. I went shopping at one of the College swap meets. I passed a booth and saw a large white telescope. I began counting my lucky stars immediately, because I had been searching for a telescope for quite some time. I had studied astronomy and telescope design in preparation for the big buy that I knew was soon to come. Only that chance was now at hand, so I would try my luck.

I approached the seller (who looked like an old fishing skipper), and remarked that it was uncommon to see one of the old "dinosaurs." He came to his telescope's defense by saying, "Hey there, that's an eight inch Cave, a powerful piece of optical equipment. Works just like it did when it was new." "And when was that?" I asked him, "In the 1960's? Because that's when it was manufactured. Meade and Celestron are the leaders today. Cave is out of business." (Which were all true statements.)

"Yeah, but look at the size of it." He pointed to the tube body that was over five feet long.

"Means nothing," I told him flatly, "Other than the fact that its focal ratio is F9 or higher. An eight inch mirror in a long tube won't gather any more light than another eight."

"A longer focal length means better detail," he tried, "You haven't seen the planets in a scope like this!"

"It means better detail, all right, for the planets, but it falls short as a deep sky performer. The field of view is much smaller in that scope." Then I went on to explain about catadioptric (mirror-lens) telescopes, versus the Newtonian types. I told him that if he prided himself on the upkeep of his scope, then why couldn't I see my reflection in its mirror (he had left the dust cap off the front of the tube opening — the mirror was grime covered). I also trifled over the age of the scope and explained to him that I would have trouble finding parts. (This was to test his knowledge of the subject. I knew that this scope's parts were interchangeable with another brand.)

After a lengthy exchange of pros and cons, I did get the scope for $400.00, a $150.00 reduction from his original asking price. This was after I had convinced him that I wanted the scope for parts only. (This wasn't entirely true. It was functional as it was. Just a mirror cleaning would remedy the problem.)

The verbal exchange between us lasted over thirty minutes in this scope purchase. It was, at times, very difficult wagering. He was not easy to convince, and he nearly turned his back on me at one point. However, I waited for a breakdown in his attitude. I waited to see if I could unnerve him — even make him tired of listening to me. In the end, I listened for a phrase, from him, that would indicate his defense weakening. It was the familiar, "Well, how much do you think that it's worth, then?" I replied, "Well, I only have $400.00 in the bank, and I don't know if I should be doing this..." So, the deal was sealed. The rest is history.

This could be called the "head to head" technique. You have to be prepared —armed with a solid knowledge of your subject. When the sparks are through flying, you might be surprised to find out that you've made a friend; someone who sincerely appreciates your interest. Give it a try, both for a profit and a friend.

Even if prices are plainly marked, you can still offer, "Well, would you consider taking $ $ $ for it?" This always works best at garage sales, of course. The sellers from the larger sponsored swap meets are a bit more fixed in their prices. They're still likely to deal if the approach is right. As a general rule, I would set my first offer at about thirty percent off the asking price and work from there. Even if it means a ten percent off victory for you in the end, it is still ten percent less than what you would have paid for it.

THE PURCHASE AND A FRIENDLY HANDSHAKE

After you have made your reduced purchase (or killing, and we hope you have), you might introduce yourself to the seller if you haven't already. Nothing seems as lonely or noncommittal as a "cold purchase," especially for the seller. A "cold purchase" is one in which a buyer succeeds in getting a reduced cost, then hurries on his way without a simple "thank you" or a friendly chat. This leaves the seller with the idea, "Well, that was all he wanted from me, just a deal."

Consider the fact that you might see this seller again. Maybe under similar circumstances. Wouldn't it be to your advantage to leave him with good thoughts of your visit? If you consider him a friend, you will spend a little time with him. He will be more receptive to you the next time that he sees you. He might even be very happy to see you. Why? Because not many people will care about him; only what he has to offer.

The seller spends most of his time answering questions, fending off rude buyers and demands, and trying to do his best at making a few dollars before he has to shut his sale down. I have made a number of loyal and trusted friends at swap meets and garage sales. I have found (I'm delighted to admit) that I have some of the most wonderful neighbors a person could ask for. Many of them were only a few houses away — I never had the courage to stop them in the street with a warm, "Hi, neighbor, how's life?" The popularity of my garage sales has provided a common bond, an excuse for our chance meetings. Even with neighbors that I have heard are shunned by others, I found them to be exactly the opposite as portrayed. They were kind and gentle sorts. People like you and me, waiting for the opportunity to talk if someone would listen.

At garage sales and swap meets, the social and cultural barriers are torn down. No one really has an image to uphold. Rather, we are all stripped naked of the need to show off or impress. We have to admit that we have gathered in force for the same purpose. Which is shopping for fun, instead of need or prestige.

Compulsive shopping can be a curse for many. It is a serious illness that affects Americans more than most. Our system is based on the principles of free enterprise. The more you make, the more you can take. Shopping garage sales, auctions, and swap meets could help some of these people realize that shopping can be fun on nickels and dimes. More importantly, the people who are found at these events are the real treasures.

So, next time you are at a garage sale or swap meet remember that the purchase that you make is not likely to cast you into the poor house, and that the people you meet share the same thoughts as you; remember to relax, get a bargain, and have fun doing it.

Chapter Five

THE PSYCHOLOGY OF THE SELLER

My, What Big Teeth You Have!

Once you have decided that a weekend garage sale is for you, then you will have to make a survey of your garage or storage area and make a list of items that you feel you could part with for some ready cash. Keep in mind that the garage is a storage place in which all family members have personal belongings. It would be wise to hold a family council to discuss what belongs to whom and its availability for sale. Once an agreement is made, and separate lists are devised for each family member, the items can be moved to a corner of the garage, away from items that will not be sold.

Do not sell items that do not belong to you. I've heard of one case in which a family inadvertently sold the belongings of a tenant who was away on vacation. When the tenant returned home three weeks later, she was shocked to find that her snow skis had been sold in the sale, for an amount considerably less than what she had paid for them. So when in doubt, exclude it from the sale. Even if the items in your garage are storage favors for some friend or neighbor.

The next question you will ask yourself will be which items hold the most value and which hold the least.

Family memorabilia such as personal photograph albums, correspondence, letters, family documents, licenses, certificates, receipts of ownership, old tax forms, wedding, birthday and anniversary announcements, romantic keepsakes, and other such items of personal interest will be of no use at all to the general public. These personal treasures should be found and removed from any and all containers, then filed away for safe keeping. A page-flattened rose from 1925 might have great meaning to you but it is worthless to the buyer who is looking for a card table.

WHAT DO YOU HAVE THAT SOMEONE WANTS?

Let's confine ourselves to some basic and popular items commonly sold at garage sales. It's a sure bet that you will have several items belonging to these categories: antique furniture, aquariums, art and decorator items, baby accessories, bathroom and plumbing supplies, household furniture, beds and mattresses, bikes, books, calculators, cameras, camping equipment, locks, clothing, computer systems, dryers and washers, exercise equipment, freezers, musical instruments, housewares, luggage, stoves, electric motors, office supplies, optical equipment, paintings, radios, gardening supplies, records, refrigerators, rugs, sewing machines, silverware, sporting goods, stereos, tape recorders, telephones, tools (hand and power), toys, typewriters, TVs, vacuum cleaners, and home video units.

Most of these items are very good sellers, some more so than others. The larger household appliances are heavy and difficult to move. It is advised that the larger items be advertised in the newspapers or trade publications. Many a hopeful purchaser for these items searches these references for such specialty items. However, some working appliances are excellent sellers and we will examine these further on in the book.

A word about theme first. A garage sale or swap meet (flea market) booth has a gender. Didn't you know that? It is male-oriented, female-oriented, or both. Since you want to attract all possible buyers it is important that you carry a male/female theme.

Typically, an adult male garage sale production would include: automobile parts, tools (hand and power), sports equipment, plumbing, air-conditioning and heating hardware, gardening equipment (small engines), exercise equipment, electrical motors, and all manner of recreational gear. You'll find an assortment of "neutral" items in the male-run sale as well.

It is not hard to spy from a car, and at a glance recognize, a male-run sale. Some of them look like miniature junk yards with a few splashes of color. Most items are dusty and grease-ridden and they are usually displayed on the ground.

Since the greatest percentage of buyers are families, this type of sale is likely to discourage a woman or young girl from approaching it. Worse, I've seen family cars cruise a male-run sale, the wife throws up her hands with disinterest, and the car continues on. What's the reason? It's not fair! And it isn't.

Conversely, when a woman decides to run a sale, the opposite happens. Women are not casual when displaying goods, for one thing. You will see more display tables in a female-run sale. Items and goods will be laid out almost precisely in neat rows. Sometimes there will be sheets and coverlets draping the tables. There is an excellent chance that you will see items marked for the exact amount with fine penmanship written on neat white tags. And you will always see more color. The color will be seen in clothes, bedding, baby accessories, plates, dishes, porcelain, household appliances, games and toys, and related articles. I've seen TVs and radios operating at female-run garage sales. I've seen chairs provided for weary shoppers and refreshments served. Ultimately, the women win hands down for the neatest, most accommodating and decorative displays. Women are also apt to be less self-conscious when putting on a sale, taking great pride in the smallest of transactions.

The men who visit these female-run sales with their wives are sure to be a little nervous and sometimes evasive when making a purchase. Stand a man between two dozen hanging garments, flank him on the other side with baby toys, and present him face to face with a platoon of flower baskets, and he will begin toe-tapping and watch-watching. He sees nothing brutal here. He feels trapped like, yes, a bull in a china shop — feeling that if he leans the wrong way he might touch something delicate. Since he might be the one carrying the expense money, the result for the wife or daughter could be catastrophic, especially when the females have their heart set on something.

What's wrong with either of these types of sales? Nothing, if it is not intended to be a serious sale. Plenty, if the intention of the sale is to make money. You will lose fifty to seventy percent of your potential sales dollars if you run a single gender type sale. I've seen it happen as I have run both types.

In one instance, with a female-run sale, I counted 141 cars passing the driveway. Only fifty-two stopped to investigate the sale, with twenty-three making purchases. In other repeated female-run sales the figures varied slightly but basically remained the same. (Take into note the day, time of the sale, and your neighborhood population density when considering this.)

In the male-run sale, I've witnessed 170 cars passing, ninety-five investigations, and sixty-two purchases. (Slightly higher.)

Solution: compromise the sales. There are two ways to do this. What I call a neutral sale is a display that has items attractive to both sexes i.e., the goods are neither male or female predominantly, but represent a comfortable mix. Strangely, these goods have a soothing effect, even striking up bonds of empathy between husband and wife. Some of these items are: household furniture, cameras and movie projectors, records, bikes, clocks, musical instruments, TVs, stereos, pictures and frames, books, children's toys, luggage, computers, typewriters, and home video units.

A good, fast selling item for both sexes is a typewriter. The common electric typewriter is such a magnet to both sexes that I often have two or three on hand to sell. They go very fast. Women are inherently good at communications skills. Many of them have honed their dexterity on typewriters at some point in their lives, whether it was at school or at the office. Men like machines, something that demonstrates power. And many men realize the practicality of such a purchase because it serves as an instructional/constructive piece of equipment. In short, it produces.

The other type of sale is the ladies to the left, gentlemen to the right. In this case lots of both male and female items are on display. To one side of the driveway you can see weight-lifting gear, fishing poles, maybe a tent, some tools and tool chests, and various pieces of sports equipment. On the opposite side of the driveway you will find the common female items: housewares and appliances, clothes, dishes, pots and pans, games, toys, statuettes, jewelry, and assorted handcrafted items and knickknacks. Perhaps in the middle of the driveway you will find some of the neutral items, to smooth out the dividing line.

Men and women need their space. They invariably separate even in grocery stores for short times. What this left/right sale does is give both partners breathing room; a chance to explore things that are of interest only to them. Men will usually rally around camping equipment, rifles and shotguns, tools, and sporting gear, discussing outdoor activities, vacation plans, or hobby interests. The ladies will congregate around eye-appealing arrangements, perhaps talking about jewelry, handicrafts, or wearing apparel.

The neutral or the left/right sale offers a fair shake to both sexes. They also top the list for the most income. Example: in a left/right sale, (a neighborhood block sale event) 275 cars passed, with 243 investigations and 220 purchases. Total income realized in a forty-eight hour period was $1,600. Many of the lost sales were due to parking problems.

FAST SELLERS – HOT ITEMS

For men, the most frequently bought items will be tools and tool chests. Tools are a valuable and practical buy for any household or automotive need. If you happen to run across a nice collection of tools and buy them as a whole with a bid purchase, you might consider selling extras or duplicates at individual prices. The most sought after tools are Snap On, Cornwell, Mac,

Matco, Craftsman, Power Craft, and Stanley, to name a few. Most of these tools are triple chrome-plated (rust resistant), and carry a lifetime warranty against breakage and poor workmanship. Black and Decker and Skill power tools are also a lasting and practical buy: drills, grinding wheels, jigsaws, saber saws, etc.

Most department store tool chests, bottom and top boxes (the more drawers the better), are outstanding sellers. Sears, Montgomery Ward, J.C. Penney, Target, and K-Mart stores sell these boxes. Secondhand, these tool chests offer great savings since a typical combination chest might run as high as $300.00. Snap On, Cornwell, Matco, and Mac boxes are of better quality (thicker gauge steel, heavier runners), so you will have to consider a higher asking price for them.

All manner of sports equipment is of great interest to men. The weight benches, rowing machines, exercise bikes, sit-up boards, and barbell and dumbbell sets are sure sellers. Camping equipment: fishing poles, tents, Coleman stoves and lanterns, rifles and shotguns are fast sellers. Note: It is not against the law to sell rifles and shotguns to a private party but I would use extreme caution and judgment in doing so. Rifles seem to be the biggest seller in the sports equipment category but selling them to minors is prohibited by law. Never sell a handgun or a knife (that could be considered a lethal weapon) at a garage sale. A concealed weapon that has been used in a felony can be traced back to you if you have not made the proper registration transfer. Play it safe when selling firearms or weapon-like merchandise. This would apply to fireworks or any other pyrotechnic device as well.

Furniture of any sort that is sturdy and presents good value, is often considered a practical buy by men. In garage sale purchasing I have noticed that the men were inclined to buy secondhand furniture for room additions, like play rooms or game rooms. Small kitchen dinettes serve well as card tables or crafts tables. Small desks with drawer space attract attention, along with bar stools or padded chairs. Redwood picnic tables can serve well as outside fixtures, or can be used as an indoor utility table or workbench.

Gardening tools like shovels, rakes, brooms, and clippers are a welcome purchase for men. They hold their value as they have few moving parts and rarely break. The motorized gardening hardware like chain saws, leaf blowers, weed trimmers, and edgers are a good bargain if in proper working order and priced accordingly. Power lawnmowers in working condition are also a good bargain for the men in the family. The cheapest rotary cutting models run around $100.00 and this is usually minus a $30.00 grass catcher.

Though bicycles are a neutral item, the men often show a greater interest in them, especially the five and ten speed models, with Schwinn being the overall favorite. It is difficult to sell secondhand bicycles at a garage sale. Over the years the prices have remained fairly constant and have even dropped further. I've seen foreign make ten speed racers for as low as $49.95 at the retail chain department stores. Your prices will have to be low. Perhaps as much as forty percent off the retail price. However, garage sale buyers will still pay up to $35.00 for a used bike.

Clothes, always a good seller

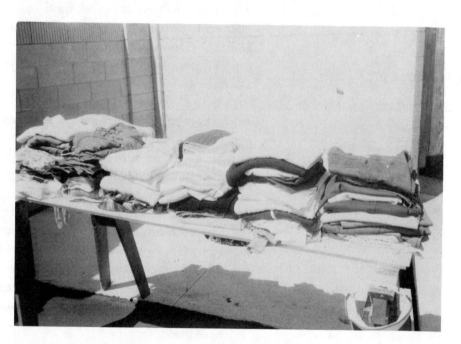

Women shoppers are still browsing through clothes — even secondhand clothes. If you have a wide selection of sizes and materials you're certain to find the lady shoppers looking for kick-around clothes for all members of her family. She looks for dresses and suits with simple lines. Anything that might indicate low upkeep and cost is a bargain to her. She'll look for coordinates that can be worn as ensembles or with other outfits. She'll pay attention to dresses or fabrics in blends of cotton and synthetic fibers which are wearable for three seasons and even in winter for casual wear. Her motto will be low upkeep and maintenance, with low cost the priority of the three considerations.

The women will also seek out polyester and cotton shirts for the men in the family. These popular shirts have seen an incredible rise in price since the late 1960's. With the advent of designer clothes the prices have shot up even further for the same brand clothing that is sold in the major retail outlets. T-shirts and sweatshirts with animal prints or logos are popular buys. If you

Garage sale clothes display

Swap meet clothes display

have suits that are of good quality with little wear expect to hang a few of these up for your sale. I will also add that clothes that are freshly laundered and pressed present the best chances for sale. Anything as intimate as clothing should be displayed above the ground and organized according to size. Furthermore, hanging up the clothes on racks or garage door rods gives shoppers the advantage of checking labels and sizes.

Pots, pans, and silverware (clean and sans dents) are popular items for women shoppers. Copper and cast iron skillets and frying pans are durable and can be used repeatedly. They are also easy to sterilize. If you have complete sets of secondhand cookware your chances of making a sale are all that much better. This would also apply to salt and pepper shakers, seasoning jars, canisters, measuring spoons and ladles, knife sets, plastic food storage containers, and other items that come in graduated sizes.

Portable electric cooking appliances, from rotisseries to broilers, are widely bought. Other popular appliances are electric can openers, blenders, toasters, warming ovens, food processors, microwaves, and knife sharpeners. GE products are carefully engineered and promise the most value for the money. Other comparable makes are Westinghouse, Presto, Farberware, Dormeyer, Hamilton Beach, and AMC. Corning ceramic cookware is also a very popular item because it is durable and very easy to clean, and it is nonporous. Crockpots and pressure cookers are other medium-sized appliances that sell well.

Ceramic and porcelain figurines, statuettes, animal figures, and dolls probably represent the largest gross (in numbers) product at any garage sale. We're talking about all of those little knickknacks, ashtrays, coin plates, and other items that can be sold for under a dollar, many of them for nickels and dimes. Figurines made of china, jade, bone, ivory, and other quality materials, always get scooped up at garage sales, and it is the women who find pleasure in these decorative pieces. Call them conversation pieces — they can include anything from a pair of brass book ends to a miniature handcarved figure of an Indian chief. If it is unique, it is sure to attract attention.

It is surprising to me how well bedding, sheets, blankets, coverlets, and comforters sell at garage sales, as well as pillows and pillowcases (in good condition), especially the down and feathered varieties. Talking with several women I discovered that most of them who had water beds in their homes were reluctant to purchase the custom bedding appropriate for such. Why? The costs were enormous!

Plain weave terrycloth towels are very popular, and if you have matching sets of raised or designer types, all the better. Remember, plain white towels are more absorbent than the fancier types. This is because they have not been deep-dyed.

Acrylic blankets like Orlon and Creslan are popular because they are machine washable. Wool costs the most but retains heat better. The polyester, cotton, and rayon blankets are the least expensive.

Low maintenance sheets made from polyester and cotton fiber are the most wanted types. They are more resilient and have greater strength than all cotton sheets. They also never have to be ironed.

Any unfaded and little worn comforter is a blessing to find. They can be extremely expensive when purchased new. If they have an attractive print or design (in any color) someone will usually consider buying it, even secondhand. Comforters are popular in summer when many people sleep with fewer blankets. They are easy and manageable when making beds, extremely durable, and last for years.

When displaying bedding it is a must that it be visibly clean, folded neatly, and perhaps covered with some type of see-through plastic to keep out dust and moisture.

Along with these men's and women's favorites, there are the neutral items discussed earlier. With a combination of these men's and women's favorites plus a variety of neutral items, you can expect to do quite well in your garage sale. These items do well at the swap meets (flea markets in which you set up your merchandise in an area or booth).

Any hobby in which you have created and mass-produced goods that you believe are potential sellers would also be included in this listing. For instance: I've sold a great many (kit) doll houses and miniatures at the large swap meets, particularly around Christmastime — a great time for theme-related arts and crafts. One lady that I know makes beautiful jewelry from seashells. Another craftsman makes and displays his own unique version of wallmounted bookshelves. I've watched another seller profit with her dazzling array of sand candles, made with different colored waxes and stylized molds. Creativity in any form that displays a unique quality is always of interest to the buyer.

VISITING OTHER SALES

Visiting other garage and swap meet sales will show you how others set up and display their merchandise. Note the items that they have on display. Ask questions concerning the frequency of their sales, the times and days, and their advertising routes. Ask them which items do the best. Ask what items have been requested from them: at swap meets customers frequently ask a regular seller about the availability of future merchandise. From the many answers that you will get, you will formulate your own strategy and be better able to succeed and deal with your competition.

There is another reason for visiting other sales. In the past I have used techniques to acquire goods that I did not have. And if you are considering using garage sales as a supplement to your income on a regular basis, you might use these techniques to build up additional stock.

I have used a technique that I call the "bid out." First, I scout different sale locations, make a note of their addresses and what items they are displaying. After this, I will determine which sale is likely to sell out the entire inventory for a lump sum. This gets a bit tricky. With practice you will be able to gauge the attitude of a seller. A seller who does not sell often and sets up in a casual manner will, more often than not, take a one-time bid for all the goods. These kinds of sales will usually be the single gender types, and the sellers themselves will demonstrate a non-serious nature, such as the owner of a home who intends to clean his garage out by donating the items to charity. Only he has second thoughts about the donation, and instead thinks, "Why not try a one day sale and pick up some extra cash?" It is really a wishful, half-hearted attitude that prompts him to decide on a sale. He doesn't really think that he has anything special to offer.

This is the type of sale that is ripe for the "bid out."

A case in point. I found the address of a sale one day and lingered curbside to watch the activity. The sale house was one of the better beachfront homes in our community and I knew for certain that this was where some of the better deals were to be found. After awhile, I approached the sale and introduced myself to the man who was tending it. I quickly scanned the goods that he had arranged on the ground. Right then, I knew that the odds were in my favor for a bid out. I also watched the man carefully. He sat on a stool in the shade of his garage, never venturing out into the sunlight, even to greet customers. My first impression of him gave him away. He was happy, jovial. Too happy. All of these factors pointed like a dagger to the reasons for the sale:

1. Even before the evidence was clear, I knew that I had a chance at some great bargains owing simply to the address of this house. It was located in the harbor area of our community. There the homes are priced upwards of $300,000. Folks who are well off can readily afford luxuries that you or I cannot. They are apt to be easier on customers when it comes to asking prices. Their situation is not desperate or dependent upon the sale. Conclusion: expendable merchandise.

2. His merchandise was grounded. There are two basic reasons for this. Either he was lazy in putting this sale together, or he did not believe that the

used and dusty items he had were good enough to be placed on tables and displayed at waist level. I ruled out the possibility that he was lazy. His home was indication enough that he had done some type of hard work in his life. Also, he had gone to the trouble of advertising the sale in the newspaper. So he had haphazardly tossed his goods on the driveway and sat back to survey the crowd. I also ruled out the idea that he did not have the tables or benches for displaying his sale. Display platforms are easily made from other household gear (we will examine this in a later chapter). Simply, there was a lack of prestige in this sale. Conclusion: poor attitude.

3. I got the distinct impression from this man that he was slightly ashamed of having to put the sale on. I was sure that he did not want to be seen openly on his driveway among his clutter. Not for all of his neighbors to see. He stayed far back into his garage and made customers come to him. Remember, it was a very wealthy neighborhood. I could understand his reluctance. He quite possibly was a doctor with a lawyer and a corporation president living on either side of him. I'm sure that he wanted to avoid that "raised eyebrow." Possibly, the motive for the sale might have come from his wife, and therefore he had bent to her wishes. Rather than junking the items as he had planned, it was suggested to him that he sell them. Whatever the true reason, the conclusion was: embarrassment.

4. He was overly friendly in a nervous type of way. He was anxious for a fast sale. He didn't appear interested in bickering over prices. He was agreeable. I could almost read this man's mind: "Buy something. Buy anything. Just as long as I can get this thing over with. It wasn't my idea. I never do this. I'll never do it again. Just buy something. Anything." Conclusion: desperation.

> Expendable merchandise
>
> + Poor attitude
>
> + Embarrassment
>
> + Desperation
>
> = Bid Out

From the moment I stepped upon his driveway and surveyed his goods, I knew that I had an excellent chance to relieve him of the whole sale. I took in all of these considerations in about thirty seconds. Only at this sale, the things that I found interesting (potential profit) were seven bicycles. So this was going to be a partial bid out.

Five of the bikes were ten speed makes. The other two were older three speeds. Incredibly, they all were twenty-six inch frame models, except one, which was a twenty-four inch. It was no surprise to me when the owner told me that they were all broken. (I could plainly see this.) He wanted ten dollars apiece for them. I told him that I would take the bunch for $30.00. He hesitated for a brief moment, but agreed to the deal. He was as eager as I was to get the bikes off of his driveway.

When I got home, I disassembled the bikes and cleaned them. From the parts I managed to assemble three very clean and shiny bicycles (in perfect working order) and store them in my garage. Two weeks later I sold one bike for $30.00 and the other two for $25.00 apiece.

You see, in bikes of the same model, style, and size all of the parts are interchangeable. It is only a matter of shifting workable parts to another frame to make a completed working model. I produced three functioning bikes out of the seven. And I still had spare parts for a nearly completed fourth. It would be a simple matter to find more of the same and repeat the process.

This was a partial bid out but I have bought entire sales for as little as $45.00. The most that I have ever paid for a complete sale is $200.00. At once, you can begin to see a tremendous profit margin. You will need a truck, van, or station wagon — a vehicle suitable for moving such vast amounts of merchandise.

Be space conscious when considering the bid out. Survey the items and make a list. Consider the potential worth of the sale — remember, you are buying everything. If the seller refuses to sell the entire sale, leave them with your phone number, along with the bid that you intend to pay. Chances are, if their sale does poorly, you can expect a call. If you are called back to the sale later in the day, note the items missing, adjust your bid, and try again. Be polite, but persistent. This is an excellent way to help stock your next garage sale.

DONATIONS

Nowadays there are a lot of hauling services around. I was always curious to know what these haulers were hauling away and how they determined their rates for load sizes and destinations. That was until I talked to some of them and found out the particulars of their business. They told me that the majority of homeowners requesting their services usually wished to dispose of refuse: tree stumps, sod, branches, leaves, weeds, bricks, rocks and stones, and discarded structures. The refuse was taken to city dumps at a moderate cost. The haulers called most of the stuff that they collected "junk." (We'll talk about that word later.) However, there were plenty of times when the refuse showed considerable value. Some of the things were: books and magazines, bicycles, lamps, compressors, lawnmowers, furniture, and other such stuffs. And when they mentioned that old furniture was a favorite throwaway item, my eyes blinked. (Furniture that was manufactured in the 18th and 19th century has been commonly mistaken for pieces made in the early 1900's.) So you can now see the reasons for my interrogations.

I won't bother you with some of the "gems" that I found as a result of dealing with these haulers on a private and personal level. The deals were sparse and few. But what led me to the next step was important. On a larger scale, I found that the freebie section of the trades and newspapers led me to a more ethical and faster approach to what I was after. I wanted something of value for nothing. And I found it in the giveaway or freebie section of the listings. I knew that I would have to make many phone calls, not to mention expend gas and time, to reach the freebie people. But I weighed the odds after several attempts, and the effort did pay off more than once. The following is a typical extract from one of the classified newspapers. The "*" indicates goods that I consider likely candidates for a garage sale.

8' Couch, dark brn, reasonable cond, you haul.*
BED, full sz, you haul.
CLEAN fill dirt, you haul.
72 EL CAMINO, minus frnt end, you haul.
ELECTRIC washer and dryer, working, you PU.
79 HONDA cvcc 1300 eng, you haul.
MODERN living rm set, grt cond, you haul.*
FILL DIRT 5-10 yards, you haul.
MICROWAVE has broken glass, wks gd, you PU.*
PALM TREE, large, you take.
62 VW Bug, call...
SANDY SOIL, you haul.
WASHER not wrking, you trnspt.
GOLF clubs, some rust, you haul.*
10' camper, you haul
2 twin sets of matts, gd cond,...
70 VW body and pan, you haul
SOIL, take all you want, call...
BRICKS 2000 lbs, you haul.
SAIL BOAT, 23 ft, nds mst, you trl.

As you can see from this listing, many of the items are large and carry considerable weight. The items that are marked with the asterisk are the ones that I would investigate, but I would not necessarily take them. The golf clubs, since they are easily cleaned, would be the best bet in this listing. I would also consider the distance that I had to travel to get them. I would travel under twelve miles to pick up such merchandise.

A simpler route for donated items, and the one that works the best, is to ask your neighbors. Someone you know is more likely to give you goods of quality. You might, as a favor, help them clean their garage in exchange for goods or any other service that demonstrates your appreciation. It will be remembered.

CONSIGNMENT AGREEMENTS

I have just started using the device of consignment agreements. It has worked rather well but I have had to screen the items, picking out goods that I thought would sell quickly. Most of the consignment agreements were with neighbors who were located in my housing tract. This way I would not have to travel far in making pickups, or sending items back to the owners. I consider a garage sale an open air market.

Notice that I said "market." I treat it as such, and I expect those who consign goods to me to be equally aware of my position. Consignment agreements can range anywhere from ten percent of the asking price on up to fifty percent. I generally charge thirty percent on goods that I have to pick up and display, and later return if not sold. If they transport their goods to and from my sale, I will charge them twenty percent. In the latter example, this frees up my time since I do not have to make several trips to the neighbors.

Chapter Six

ADVERTISING: NEWSPAPERS, FLYERS, SIGNS

My, What A Big Mouth You Have!

Nobody is going to know that you are having a sale if you don't tell them. The quickest way to announce your intentions is through advertising. Advertising must work since so many corporations pay out millions for it, ranging from simple flyers or handbills to prime time radio and television spots. It is the surest way to reach a mass audience. The corporations know this. They have found that advertising pays. They know that by the law of averages they will be able to recover their investment, because enough consumers will find an interest in their product. The only way that the corporations would suffer a loss would be if they failed to know and use the proper advertising routes. Selecting the proper method of advertising is a strategy in itself. Employees in large corporations are handpicked and paid generous salaries and bonuses just to come up with ideas to better their firms' chances of financial gain.

You will use different methods in getting your message out to the public. Your routes will be less expensive. And it is unlikely that you will ever be sued for false advertising or misrepresentation. In short, advertising for garage sales is risk free. Your total advertising might cost as little as $10.00. Certainly, no more than $50.00 is needed to get the word out. A reasonable amount to spend on garage sale advertising is around $22.00. You have merely to make reservations with a newspaper office, at least one to two weeks in advance, supplying them with the information you have on your sale — the articles for sale, the days and times.

Advertising is the MOST IMPORTANT aspect of the sale itself. Any sale. This applies to auctions, sidewalk sales, rummage sales, swap meet sales, estate sales, moving sales, yard sales, liquidations, block sales, and our common garage sale. It can make your sale a whopping success or a dismal failure. Without advertising, it *will* be a dismal failure. It cannot be stressed enough. Do you want to reach dozens of customers — or thousands? You have to remember that for every twenty people who read your ad notice, perhaps only one of them will show up. You need the odds in your favor. It's kind of like shooting for Mars and hitting the moon. If your advertising effort is on a colossal scale, your chances for a lucrative sale are great. If your effort in advertising is great, your sales are bound to be good. If your effort is good, your chances for profit will be fair. A fair advertising effort begets poor results. Poor efforts in advertising are certain to produce little if any sales at all.

Regular businesses and shops need to advertise frequently. This is a standard practice in the business field. They must see to it that they are listed in as many sources as they can afford, sometimes including radio time and yellow page listings. If they can continually advertise, don't you think that you can expend the effort to give it everything you've got, just once?

NEWSPAPERS AND SHOPPING MAGAZINES

When advertising in newspapers, generally the city newspapers are large enough to notify an audience of your plans to run a sale. The circulation in such newspapers might be anywhere from 10,000 to 100,000, depending upon the subscribers to the paper.

The ad rates that you will pay will vary according to the policy of the paper, the area that you wish to reach, and the word count, or size of your ad. You may pay around a dollar per word, sometimes twice that amount. Many times you will pay for a block of twelve words, or fifteen words, or twenty words for a fixed price. Thereafter (if your ad is larger), you will pay a slightly reduced rate for each word, or group of words. Find out exactly what the newspaper's rates are and if you are entitled to any special rate. Many newspapers have bargain months or occasions when they lower their advertising costs.

The number of people who will see your ad in newspapers is only limited by the circulation (distribution size) of the newspaper itself. If you want to reach a larger audience, increasing your chances for sales, you could check out ad space in one of the larger county editions. In advertising in the city or county newspapers, you want the "dailies," those papers that publish editions every day of the week. It would not make sense to advertise in a weekly or monthly newspaper unless your ad was sure to run before and near your sale.

You should know that a county newspaper will reach many of your surrounding cities. Some of these cities might be as much as fifty miles away. Rarely will anyone travel that distance for a county flea market, much less a garage sale. But county newspapers will saturate the heavily populated cities that surround yours, so it's not a bad bet. The additional $10.00 spent would increase your ad exposure tenfold.

You can see a typical ad listed below. This ad was placed in our own *Orange County* (CA) *Register.*

85 FORD RANGER w/service body, very clean, low miles, like new — $6,500

This ad runs around twelve words. It cost $18.00 to run this ad for seven days in a row. The county newspaper was notified a week in advance when the ad was placed.

Another example could look like this:

GARAGE SALE books, office equipment, toys, sporting goods, clothes, jewelry, everything goes. (Phone number here.)

If you are advertising a two day garage sale, you might call up for ad space two weeks in advance. Specify that the ad run five days prior to the sale and finish on the last day of the sale, for a total of seven days running. That makes it five days directly before the sale and two days during. If it is a one day sale you would run six days prior and one day during, for the seven day ad.

Always reserve space in advance. This will give you plenty of time to cancel the ad if you happen to have an emergency, or find that your plans have changed. Many times a newspaper will cancel an ad and give you a partial refund if you have sold an item before the ad expires. This will also save you unnecessary phone calls about an item that you have already sold.

The shopping magazines or rags as they are commonly called, specialize in selling ad space. That is all they do, and therefore they almost have it down to a science. Some of these shopping magazines are enormous and carry great volumes of information. Some of the largest ones are alphabetized and include easy to find indexes. Items can be listed under codes, blocks or sections.

Many of these magazines use clip art (symbols) to denote what kind of a sale it is. The small silhouette of a car or a boat might be placed next to the ad to draw attention to the fact that this is a car or boat ad only. Thus a reader can visually skim through the pages for a specialty item and easily find it. These symbols, such as a silhouette of a star or a pointing finger, cost more. For a couple of dollars extra these symbols help flag your ad. It makes the reader think that the non-flagged ads are full in comparison, and this is exactly what they are supposed to do.

Shopping magazines like ours, the *Penny Saver* (one of the largest), and the *Super Saver* cost a bit more per ad than the city and county newspapers. There is a precise reason for this. The shopping magazines sell ad space by zones. Typically, a city of 100,000 population will have six zones. For instance, they would be called (central) Townville, (north) Townville, (northwest) Townville, (south) Townville, (southwest) Townville, and (southeast) Townville. You can see that our fictional city of Townville is divided up into six zones. Smaller cities with half the population and area of Townville might have only three zones, and so on.

Shopping magazine zones

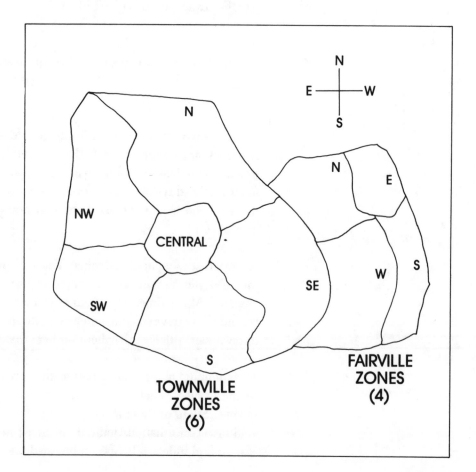

A typical shopping magazine ad request form will state the number of words that you are allowed to use, and list the available zones that you can advertise in. You will be charged a flat rate for this small initial ad. You can run a longer ad but it will cost slightly more. Below is an example of an ad guideline.

12 WORDS-8 LOCAL ZONES $12 (per week)
Longer ads, each 4 words 50 cts per zone
(please do not abbreviate)

In our city called Townville, you can already see that six zones will be used in it, with two additional zones left over. In the shopping magazines there will be a list of additional cities and zones to choose from. You could pick two more zones from a nearby city. Then you will have advertised in two cities, in this case saturating Townville and advertising partially in another.

You will soon find that advertising in shopping magazines can be downright fascinating when you realize that you will have to know your community and surrounding cities. You will have to know what part of your city is densely populated and what part is not. You will become community conscious, finding that there are affluent sections of your city, sections that are mostly industrial, and sections that are middle class and residential. If you know that a zone in your city has a 100 acre park and that the population around it is sparse, you would be wise to buy a different zone.

Let's suppose that Townville is a real city with a population of 100,000 residents. It is an average city by general standards, and we have the eight zone package for $12.00. Common sense tells us that we will use up six of the zones in our home city since our customers are that much nearer to us. We also think that the six zones in our city are good prospects. We have two zones left, and we want to purchase four more zones. Our cost for the four additional zones will be $6.00, or $1.50 per extra zone (our ad reads twelve words). Now we have to decide on where our other six zones will go. We know that they will be as close to Townville as possible. We will be selling mostly exercise equipment in our sale: some bikes, a rowing machine, a bench press, a sit-up board, a set of barbells and dumbbells, a rowing machine, tennis rackets, footballs, baseball equipment, jogging clothes, an exercise bike, some golf clubs, archery equipment, and some other small sporting goods. We also have some small appliances, clothes, and children's books.

We will consider a city next to us called Fairville. We like this city because we know that it has a large city treasury and that the streets, parks, and other city development programs are better than any of our other surrounding cities. We know that in Fairville (according to the shopping magazine zone chart) the city has four zones: a north, south, east, and west.

In the west side of Fairville, we know that there is a huge retirement community with large sections of land designated for mobile home living. In the east side of Fairville we know that a large aerospace plant has just been installed, and the surrounding neighborhood is new tract homes, with some of the houses still under construction. In the north side of Fairville is where much of the city's population lives, and there are many small businesses and shops in that area. In the south zone we know that the entire area is populated with new computer-related corporations and industry plus a large residential section. The south zone is also suburban; there are hills, winding roads, and more timberland.

Since we have mostly medium exercise equipment and some sporting goods, we are going to spend one of our zones in south Fairville. The reason is that we have examined the area and know that the employees who are working in the computer industries are in their 20's, 30's, and 40's. We know that they are a physically active bunch because we have seen dozens of them riding their bicycles to work, jogging, and indulging in lots of outdoor activities. We know for a fact that there are more health clubs in south Fairville because we have seen the club ads in the telephone directory. And since computer corporations are mostly comprised of offices, we suspect that the office workers would be likely to pursue more physical interests. Most of their working days are spent indoors sitting behind desks.

Our next choice for a zone would be the north zone. Here much of the general population lives: families, ordinary businesses, and some small factories. We could assume that we would draw a good general interest crowd here. This would help us with the rest of the sale items that we have.

The west side of Fairville (the retirement community) would not be a good choice for us. We are selling items that require physical exertion. Senior citizens (and all of us who are growing older) slow their activity down in the later years. Seniors do like recreational items, but we do not have many of these items. We have items that require vigorous exercise.

The east side of Fairville (the new aerospace plant and homes) would have been perfect if we were selling furniture and tools. Certainly, new tenants are looking for household-related stuff, even gardening tools or carpentry hardware. Since we really had none of those things, we had to pass on that zone. What we are left with is two more zone purchases: the north and the south zone of Fairville. We have four more zones left so we will pick another neighboring city and examine it like we did Fairville. If we find two more good prospects in this other city, we can buy another two zones. Then we can try another city. Or perhaps the next city we look at has six zones, and four of the zones look really good. Then we can spend our remaining four zones there.

With a little practice, detective work, and trial and error, a seller will be able to pinpoint the best zones for the merchandise that he has. If the seller has assembled a large neutral sale and he wishes to know what zones are the big responders, he will have to use common sense.

Check out the city populations. If the city is large enough it will be listed in the *World Almanac.*

Scouting the different areas of your city will familiarize you with the locations of your industrial complex, parks, schools, residential areas, and areas that are under development. Every city has a heart that beats differently. After awhile you will begin to feel the pulse of your city and the cities or area around you. Nothing can be more fascinating than knowing who really lives around you.

The shopping magazines come in two varieties: the magazine that has a cover price and does not charge for ad space, and the magazine that is free for the taking but does charge for ads. I've never had great success with the magazine that cost me a dollar. You would think that this was the best way to advertise since the ad space was free. Sorry, there are just too many people who get in on this publication; their pages seem endless, and the typeface is so small it is hard to read. I'm sure that many will disagree with me, but I have gotten better response every time that I have paid for the ad. When I know that people like me are placing ads in the same publication, I'm assured that we will all be eager to buy the listing just to check and see if our ads were correct. Those who do not want to pay for ad space are usually the types who won't even buy the paper when it comes out the next week with their printed ad. It's funny, but I guess that you get as you give.

Finally, when considering zones: it is ridiculous for you to think that any ethnic or minority factor will have a direct bearing on your sale success. I have never seen one particular race, color, or religious denomination buy more, or less, of a product. The key phrase to remember is, "Every type of person on this earth likes to spend a little money on a good bargain." You can put a label on this type of person. They're called human beings. A close friend of mine remarked to me one day, "Why is it that I never, ever get a response out of our central district? They're stingy. That's what it is! I pay good money on advertising to run my sale and they never come. They're stingy!" I calmly reminded him that in our city's central district we have about 3000 acres of horses and oil wells.

BILL & REITA

Are Happy To Sponsor
6th Neighborhood
GARAGE SALE
Saturday, May 7th.
8:00 am to 4:00 pm

We Support You!
Thanks For Supporting Us.

Must call by April 30th. to be published on map of sales sites

Call To Reserve A Sign

Be Sure To 'Ask for Bill & Reita'

for ALL Your REAL ESTATE Needs!

BILL GUZZARDO

REITA HUDDLESTON

One of our block sale sponsors' flyers.

FLYERS

Flyers are a great way to advertise in your immediate area. You can design your own advertising flyers on a plain white sheet of typing paper. You can stencil it, type it, draw it, or have someone with artistic talent make one for you. You can buy nice plastic stick-on letters from a stationery store, giving your flyer a professional touch. Anything goes: colored paper, fancy borders, or even a computer printout with a software program designed for making advertising flyers. Be as creative as you want, but remember one thing. Just make sure you title it GARAGE SALE in large, prominent letters at the top of the page. That phrase says it all. Sure, if you want, list the items that you have for sale. Just don't forget to list your address and phone number, with the times and date of the sale. You might even sign your name to the ad flyer. This gives it a nice personal touch. After you have finished creating your flyer (the master copy) you can take it to a copying service and have it reproduced for about four cents a copy.

Now that you have a couple dozen flyers, where are you going to put them? Where the most billboards are. On one college campus I counted seven triple-sided billboards. That's twenty-one advertising surfaces, and there was plenty of room on all of them. I would tack seven flyers here, one to each board. Most laundromats have tack boards nowadays. Tack up flyers in four or five of them. The supermarkets often have boards or nice advertising panels, complete with slots that hold four by five cards. You could fill out some cards here. Virtually anywhere you can find an announcement board you can hang a flyer. I've even had success displaying flyers in libraries and city parks. When in doubt ask permission to display your flyers on a facility, especially on private property. Display your flyers in areas that are designated for them. The sides of walls, buildings, store front windows, and other private property is not the place to advertise (without permission). Store owners can take great offense when they find personal ads securely taped to their window fronts.

SIGNS

Signs for your sale can be made from large pieces of cardboard or paper stock. You will use these larger signs to display at the entrances to your housing tract or in the vicinity of your neighborhood. The signs should be large enough to hold printed letters that can be easily seen from a distance or from a passing car. A 24 "by 24" sign is large enough to be seen clearly from about fifty yards. White signs with black lettering are the easiest to spot and read at a glance. Again, the phrase GARAGE SALE should be printed prominently on the sign, along with the sale location and time. Including an arrow at the bottom of the sign will help people determine in which direction your house lies. Make sure that the signs are secured very firmly to your location site. The wind can easily blow them down or twist them around to face in another direction.

*Store bought garage sale
sign*

You should display these signs at all available entrances to your housing
tract or neighborhood streets. Even a few out on the major intersection near
your home would let passing traffic know that there was a sale in the area.
Ask permission before you tape or secure the signs to walls, trees, or
telephone poles. In some cities there is an ordinance that prohibits the use of
advertising on city-owned property. In particular, telephone poles. It seems
that everybody does it anyway, because they always seem to get away with
it. But have you ever looked at a telephone pole that was used frequently for
ads and posters? It is littered with staples, wire, tape, and large nails.
Evidence that no one wanted to clean up after themselves. Just ask any line
repairman about what he thinks about climbing these poles. They are not
only an embarrassment to the city, but can be quite an eyesore to the
public.

The abused telephone pole

BANNERS

Some of the best banners that I have seen are the ones that have been produced on computers. Actually, it is the use of fan-fold printer paper in conjunction with a dot matrix printer and a software program that will allow you to make these highly professional advertising beacons. The banners can run any length, from 3' to 20', or more. It all depends on where you separate the pages. All you need is a computer with a dot matrix printer, and of course, the program (floppy disk) that will design the art work. One such software program is PRINT MASTER. This program will allow you to print any size letters lengthwise across continuous feed fan-fold paper. The program comes with 100 pieces of clip art and over 111 graphic modes. It can produce pictures, borders, and handle any other layout that you can dream up. If you do not have a computer, some print shops will design custom banners for you in this fashion. If you don't have access to a computer and can't afford the cost of a print shop banner, you can purchase banner or advertising stock at a crafts or stationery store. This paper will be thick and come on rolls. You can then hand brush your letters with paint or use felt-tipped markers to write your message. You can achieve any effect that you want: hand rendering, stenciling, adhesive letters. You might want to add some fancy borders, or include some unique patterns and designs in the lettering.

Banners are large and attract a lot of attention. They are easily read from a distance. They are most used on smooth walls where they can be taped to the surface easily. Banners are very popular at block party garage sales. A banner covering every entrance to a housing tract, in which seventy homes are displaying garage sales, is quite a thrilling event. Such advertisements leave little doubt in the public's mind as to what kind of activity is going on in the neighborhood. When banners are displayed near streets that carry heavy traffic, the response can be so enormous that you'll wish you hadn't put them up in the first place! Banners, definitely a seller's best friend, can actually draw more customers than all of the other advertising routes combined. If you decide that banners are for you, remember that you will not need some of the signs. The signs that you would use are arrow signs only, to help with directions.

HOW LONG SHOULD IT RUN?

In the case of newspapers and shopping magazines, an ad that runs for a week prior to and during the sale is quite sufficient. Two weeks will not really boost the sales potential enough to warrant the additional cost of advertising.

Flyers can be displayed a week in advance with good results. Signs and banners are best displayed a day before and the day of the sale. It is not necessary to post these any sooner. If they are left up too long they can be torn down by a passerby, or the weather can ruin their appearance; wind rain, sun-fading, etc.

Equally as important as putting the flyers, banners, and signs out there is the absolute need of taking all of them down. Jot down a small list of the locations where you have left your advertisements. This way, you will remember where they are so that you can retrieve them. You might use them again. Don't leave any signs out there after the sale is over. If the signs have your address on them, a perturbed resident will surely have some words with you. To leave your signs hanging where you left them is littering. Be mindful of others' property.

My advertising campaign will look like the example below.

1. Ad space in one county newspaper.
2. Ad space in one (preferably two) shopping magazines.
3. Two dozen flyers (invitational).
4. Five signs (invitational and directional).
5. Five banners.
Approximate cost — $20 to $28.

With this type of campaign you can relax in the knowledge that you have done a good job in getting the word out. You are guaranteed a full showing. The success of your sale will depend upon how well you are prepared to accept the masses. Your next greatest concern will be how well you present yourself and your merchandise. Without a great presentation, you're cooked. Presentation is the second most important stage of your sale. Now read on, and let's dig into this subject of superior presentation and salesmanship.

Chapter Seven

PRESENTATION AND SALE SETUP
Grandma's House

An attractive sale that is run at a convenient time is sure to be a winner. A seller who has gone to the trouble and expense of advertising his sale will want the public to be pleased with the way he has displayed his goods. With a few arrangement techniques a seller can create the illusion that his customer is about to enter a small open air market. We can call them little bazaars, for that is what they are. You can create small aisles using display tables just like you would see in a supermarket sidewalk sale. By shifting the position of the tables you can create an arena with a "horseshoe" design. You can fashion tables and platforms into wide "V" patterns or any other design that suits your fancy. The trick for you will be to design your sale setup in the most eye-appealing manner. This will add an important element to the sale itself, the element of dignity.

BEST SALE DAYS AND TIMES

In Chapter 4 we discussed the various days and times best suited to the buyer. Essentially, the times and days for the buyer will also hold true for the seller, with a few important exceptions. The foremost exception will be the exclusion of Friday as a selling day. A single gender (feminine) sale might do well enough to pay for the effort of putting it up. Many homemakers are free in the early morning, afternoon, and evening on Fridays. But a large neutral sale would suffer a loss of momentum since roughly half of the customers (the men) would not be present to participate. Monday through Friday is an excellent choice for the ladies to hold their specialty get-togethers and parties. These are the Tupperware, lingerie, Avon, Amway, and other events that are specifically held for the benefit and interest of women. A garage sale is a far cry from these types of events, though. A garage sale is larger in items, it is held outdoors, and its intention is to attract both sexes, including children.

The number one candidate for a garage sale is Saturday. It always has been, and always will be, the most lucrative day of the week. A seller who prepares for a Saturday sale must beat the buyer out of bed! This means very early in the morning, 4:00 AM to 5:30 AM, at least. Procrastination or putting it off for a few more hours in favor of some more shuteye will take money out of your pocket. I've seen too many false starts, in which even the most serious sellers have put their sale off until nine or ten, and ended up with lost revenue. Setting up at midmorning creates frustration and confusion for the buyer as well as the seller. Here you are in a frantic dash to get your goods unboxed, prepared, and displayed in an organized fashion, and the people are as thick as jackstraws, weaving in and out of the merchandise before you have even had the chance to arrange it or tag it. You will end up stumbling over your goods, answering dozens of questions, avoiding collisions with customers, and quite possibly, making a nervous fool out of yourself. This will lead to anger, and before you know it, you will be snapping at customers simply because you know that you are behind schedule, and there's not a thing that you can do about it. And if you've had your heart set on this sale, there is no surer way to start it off on the wrong foot, only because you were not awake in time to prepare it. It can pop your attitude balloon and ruin the rest of the day. Don't risk it. Be up in time.

Sunday is a fine day for a sale, too. The customer traffic will be lighter, but you can expect a fine turnout since this day is a bigger non-working day than Saturday. They won't come in droves like for a Saturday sale, and there are a few reasons for this. First, many people attend church and other religious affairs on Sunday. Simple arithmetic will tell you that your showing will be less. Secondly, many seasoned buyers will know that a Sunday sale is the second sale day in a two day or weekend sale. They naturally assume that all of the best merchandise has been sold, and the pickings will be slim. Even if you have restocked your inventory with fresh items, the general public will not know it or believe it. So how will you outfox the public and make them believe that your Sunday sale will be just as large as your Saturday sale? Real simple. Take down the banners, signs, and flyers that you have put up, and replace them with signs that read "GARAGE SALE — SUNDAY ONLY." This is a bit sneaky perhaps, especially if your original lettering said, "GARAGE SALE — SATURDAY AND SUNDAY." Those who read your signs and appeared on Saturday will blink in amazement when they see these revised editions. They're sure to forgive you for this sly maneuver. Of more importance will be what you have done out on the streets, in the stores, campuses, laundries, and wherever you originally posted your first signs. Automobile and foot traffic always changes. You will be waving a flag to new prospects, that says, "Hey folks, I'm having a Sunday ONLY sale here!" There won't be much you can do about changing your newspaper and shopping magazine ads on such short notice — they will read as they were written. What you have done though, is give yourself that slight edge in pumping up your second day to do as well as your first day. It is enough of a hook to get people to come to your sale who would not have showed up at all. Remember that professional buyers are attracted to one day sales. You'll pick up this extra traffic as well!

It goes without saying that times of bad weather — rain, sleet, snow, and heavy winds, are not good times for a sale. People are not likely to brave the elements for an important appointment, much less a garage sale held outdoors. Are there some weekends in the spring and summer months that do better than others? Yes, there are. Memorial Day, Independence Day (4th of July), and Labor Day are great choices for garage sales, as well as auctions, swap meets, liquidations, and moving sales. The weather is agreeable (in most cases) on these days — it brings the people out into the fresh air and sunshine. There is something festive about these holidays, people are in good cheer, their outlooks are brighter. Though many people vacation on these weekends, the crowd turnout for sales is still larger in comparison with the other weekends. Most of the large retail department and grocery stores run huge advertising campaigns during these celebrations. Other than Christmastime, these summer months are the largest consumer months out of the year.

As a whole, the winter and fall months will not do as well as the spring and summer. Even some days in the spring and summer months are not good sale weekends. For instance: Mother's Day, Father's Day, Passover, and Easter Sunday are slow with sales. These holidays are times of reflection where family members and relatives gather for visiting and group dinners. Easter Sunday does not do well at all for garage sales. This is a stay-at-home day.

During the Christmas holidays can be a terrific time for sales if your merchandise is theme related. Arts and crafts creations that are handmade, or new wholesale items that are decorative and appropriate as Christmas gifts, can sell quickly; not used merchandise. People are reluctant to buy garage sale type goods for family members during this holiday. If you were selling from a swap meet booth on a regular basis two weeks prior and up until Christmas, you could do extremely well with Christmas theme-type gifts. I'll never forget my miniature dollhouse campaign that I launched one Christmas. I sold nineteen models in two days, a week before Christmas day. My total take was a hefty $3,900. I admit that it took me four months to build them, but this was my profit after the investment. I saw one smart lady sell out in one day — she had made reindeer faces, complete with antlers, out of socks!

PRESENTING MERCHANDISE

If I have a regular ten speed bicycle that is in perfect working condition, and if it is caked with grease, dirt and mud, not to mention rusty, I can expect to get half of its secondhand value if I sell it in that condition. I've used this item as an example but it applies to ALL merchandise, regardless of how unkempt or old it is. I would thoroughly wash the bike, tighten the working parts, shine up the chrome, and even paint it, if necessary. Someone once remarked to me that all of that work takes the fun out of a garage sale. It will take some of the fun away from the sale, but it will double the profits. The eye is the most valuable sensory organ a human uses. Something that offends or assaults the eye triggers a negative response in the brain. The message sent is one that is undesirable, displeasing, negative. Salespersons and promoters call this "packaging." You can see the same result in a person who is illkept — ungroomed, unwashed, and slovenly. Their packaging is bad. We're likely to turn away from this type of person, as we would have the bicycle.

There hasn't been a product made that cannot be cleaned or detailed to make it appear more presentable. Automobile dealerships have detailing departments that specialize in cleaning, painting, and touching up used cars. Without this kind of service, the dealership would find it impossible to sell used vehicles. The detailers themselves are such masters that you would swear that they were adding new parts to the cars. The magic used comes in the form of a little steel wool, masking tape, and paint.

By the same token you can clean up any items that you have for sale. The most effective universal cleaner I have found is the kitchen soap pad. Brillo and SOS pads are the two most popular brands. When these pads are used with spray cleaners, such as 409 or Fantastik, the results can be impressive. The pads can often remove scuff marks from plastic and wood furniture without damaging the surface. The fine wool strands remove rust from metallic objects such as steel and iron, with even better results on chrome. Steel wool should not be used on plastic glass (plexiglass) products, like clock faces and phonograph covers. Steel wool scratches these surfaces, along with aluminum and copper. Using a warm, soaped sponge is recommended on these materials.

Once items are scrubbed thoroughly, you can use a wet towel to damp rinse them. This will remove any film. After this, use a dry cotton towel to buff them until they show a luster. Items that have a nice shine or gleam are attractive to the eye. This effort that you expend will be well worth the profits. Anything that appears new always has a better chance for sale.

Let's suppose that now you have stockpiled all the various items that you wish to sell. This would include your donations from neighbors, a number of consignment items, plus anything that you have bought using the bid out. All of the items are clean. Before you decide that the items are ready for display tables, go through this simple checklist:

1. Do you have new batteries installed in all of the appliances that use them? Are the items functioning?
2. Do you have gasoline for small motorized engines?
3. Do you have sufficient electrical outlets and extension cords to demonstrate items that use them?
4. Do you have light bulbs (small and large) installed in the sale items that use them?
5. How about some glue and tape for fast repairs?
6. Do you have price tags?
7. If you want to use them, business cards?
8. A record book for keeping track of sales and a receipt book for those who require them?

Rectangular folding table

If you do have all these things taken care of, you are going to be ready to set up your merchandise on display platforms and tables. Some of the best tables used for garage and booth sales are the long rectangular metal tables that have folding legs. These tables are about six feet long, hinge in the middle and the legs fold up into the frame. They can hold over a hundred pounds of items and remain stable, so long as they are not loaded beyond capacity. These tables are lightweight, averaging around twenty pounds. They can be folded up in a 24 x 36 x 3 inch storage size. They come equipped with carrying handles and can be carried in suitcase fashion. Six to eight folding tables like these will take up no more room than a large cardboard box, when stored. It takes fifteen seconds to set one up. They cost from $15 to $25 apiece. A large hardware store should have these in ample supply.

Thirty-six inch by thirty-six inch card tables are also great for holding displayed goods. The tops of these tables are one piece in design. The legs lock into position and fold into the frame for storage. They can be bought for as little as $10 to $15 at hardware stores. Some drug stores even carry them.

Card tables

Folding or snap-leg TV trays are fine when lined up side by side in a long row. A sheet or blanket can be stretched over them giving the appearance of a long running table. Heavy objects should never be placed on TV trays. The construction is flimsy and they are likely to buckle under weight exceeding thirty pounds. Arrange light items on TV trays, like cameras and other flat-profiled objects. They are not the place for flower urns, china, crystal, and other delicate pieces — one bump and objects can tumble from them and break.

Any other tables that you have could be used as display surfaces. A picnic table would serve fine as a steady platform. Heavier objects can be placed on these tables since their construction is better. All rectangular tables with a flat top surface are ideal candidates for display.

The whole idea in using tables in a garage sale is to keep as many items off the

"A" frame table supports

"X" bar clothes rack

ground as possible. Displaying items at waist level is convenient for the public. Things are easier to reach and handle. Items that are strewn over the ground are a hazard for foot traffic. The last thing you want is someone tripping over something that you want to sell to them. Also, people have a hard time seeing objects that are more than six feet away — no joke, that's what glasses are for.

Trash can table

If you don't have any display tables you can make them. Two metal or plastic trash cans, turned upside down, form a very steady platform. Upon them you can place two slats of wood and have a foundation on which to display. A simple covering over this makeshift table will hide the fact that you improvised.

Single trash can table

Sawhorses can be used to support large squares of plywood. Two sawhorses and a standard 4 foot by 8 foot sheet of quarter inch plywood will hold and display lots of inventory. If you don't have sawhorses, or the time to make them, you can buy kits. These kits contain metal jaws that are designed to bite and hold onto different lengths of standard two by four foot lumber. The lumber has only to be cut in two size lengths: one length for the top support piece and one length for the leg length. In all, ten sections of 2 by 4 are required to make two sawhorses. When you are through using the sawhorses, they can be disassembled for easy storage.

Two household chairs or bar stools can be mounted with planks of wood. The length of the platform is only determined by the length of the wood planks.

Another nice touch when considering extremely warm days is to provide your customers with a sun canopy. You will see these sun canopies used frequently at the swap meet/fléa market events. They are becoming more and more popular. The area under the canopy is often much cooler than the surrounding air. The shade also cuts down on glare. Glass and chrome-plated objects can reflect direct sunlight up into your eyes; this can be quite uncomfortable. Canopies are constructed of light canvas, they have aluminum frames and can be put up in a matter of minutes. The large retail hardware stores would have these canopies in stock.

Sun canopy at a swap meet

Since the first observation point of your garage sale will be from the street, you will place display platforms and tables for maximum viewing. Placing tables end to end (not parallel to the street) on your driveway or lawn, will drastically cut down on your viewing area. It would be like looking at a knife blade edge-on. If you turn the blade ninety degrees you will begin to see more of the blade surface. So it works with display tables that hold several items deep on the surface. Of course, anyone standing on your driveway or lawn will see the depth of your tables. Slow moving car traffic might not. Your first impression will be made from the street traffic. People in slow moving cars will make very quick decisions in determining the quality and size of your sale. It's either, "Hey, that looks great," or "Naw, let's pass on this one."

For the best results, tables should be placed lengthwise across your sale area. This means parallel with your street. There are a number of ways that you can place them. Tables placed in formation will yield more viewing area and save more driveway space. Tables that are placed parallel to the street but are in multiple in-line rows will give the illusion that only one table is present. Multiple rows are okay but the idea is to open up or spread the display using small angles instead of sharp corners. Multiple rows are the only alternative for swap meet vendors since the area that they are confined to is small. Swap meet vendors do not have to worry about distant traffic. You will, with garage sales. A number of table formations are possible to allow for maximum viewing. With different driveway designs lots of formations are possible.

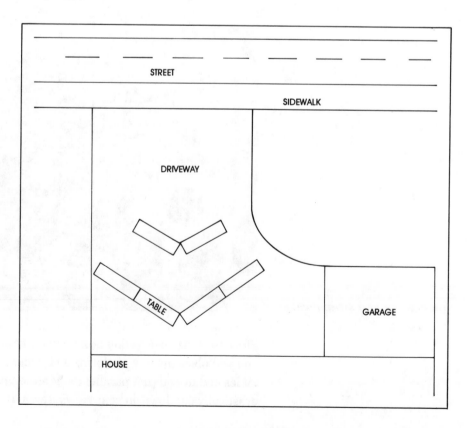

The open "U" design table formation

The horseshoe, or open "U" design, will work best with a narrow or deep driveway. A small open "U" will require just three tables: one center table and two end tables angled toward the street. The angles can run in the opposite direction to form a wedge design. Right away you can see that the tables placed at angles save driveway space, but only sacrifice a little viewing area. With a wider driveway, more center tables can be used.

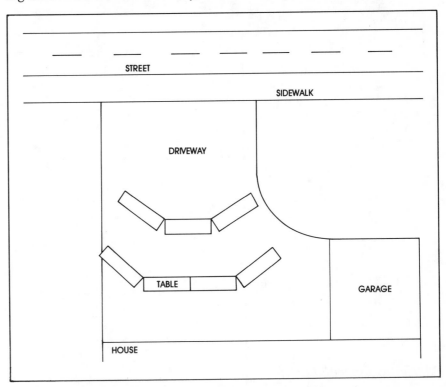

The open "V" design table formation

The "V" design can be used effectively. Four tables arranged in V formation can give you a wide viewing area. There will also be a little nook or space at the point of the V. This can be used as a vantage point for the seller. A chair or bar stool would do nicely here.

In both of these formations, the seller can sit behind the barricade, thus able to watch over goods and talk to customers. Both formations can be further expanded by adding another "U" or "V" section, inside of the other. Six tables can produce a double "V". Seven tables can produce a double "U".

If you have to place heavy items on the ground (and you will), such as bowling balls, lawnmowers, vacuum cleaners, large appliances, and exercise equipment, you would place them on tarps or blankets, in the crook of the V or U. With a single row of tables the grounded items would be placed in front of the tables toward the street.

Bicycles or tricycles are best parked near the sidewalk on the edge of the driveway. Arrange them side by side, and about two feet apart. Turn them slightly to show a three-quarter profile. Bicycles that are close to the sidewalk are easy to mount and test ride. Never lay them down on the driveway or lawn. They can be tripped over. If they have kickstands, put them down. If not, lean them against a tree or structure.

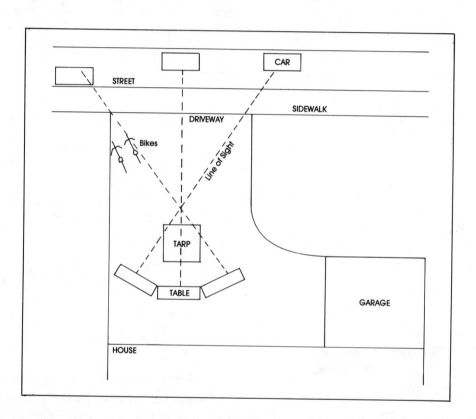

"U" formation with line-of-sight

The angle placement of the tables serves another purpose other than saving space. It affords traffic the opportunity to see tables in their line of sight. Traffic approaching from a distance will see the full profile of an angled table, but when it is directly in front of the driveway, the same table will appear at an angle.

Think up your own table formations using the small angle method. Consider trees or obstructions that are in your way. Keep your driveway and the street area directly in front of your house free of your own personal vehicles. Park them down the street a good distance from the sale. That will give customers more room for their cars. If your driveway is too small to accommodate your sale items and tables, shift some of the goods over to your open lawn area. A flat mowed lawn is not as stable as the driveway surface but it will serve the same purpose.

INVENTORY

For records' sake, you might like to take inventory of your stock before you begin the sale. This will help you keep a running account of the items that you start with, and those that are eventually sold. You can create this inventory list on a standard lined notebook pad, recording the item (brief description), the price that you expect to get for it (high and low), and the table on which it appears. Let's say that you have an older model Vivitar 35 mm camera. You know that it works because you have taken some recent pictures with it. You have the carrying strap, the case, and the instruction manual. Let's say that you are using the single open "U" formation of tables. You have one left angle table, a center table, and a right angle table. Counting your tables from left to right, you notice that your camera is on table number one, the left angle table. On your first inventory page, which is the table one page, you could list the item like this:

TABLE 1				
Item	**Make/Model**	**Condition**	**Low**	**High**
Camera, 35 mm	Vivitar w/ case, strap	man-wrking	$30	$40

For the rest of the items on table one, you might want to alphabetize.

TABLE 1				
Item	**Make/Model**	**Condition**	**Low**	**High**
Camera, 35 mm	Vivitar w/ case	man-wrking	$30	$40
Dog, porcelain fig.	import, France	good	$5	$8
Encyclopedia set	children's, complete	Britannica	$70	$90
Gun	toy, Mattel	good	$2	$3
Ice trays	set of 4	good	$1	$2
Lamp, desk type	GE	wrk	$12	$15
Molds	jello, set of 6	good	$3	$4
Oven, convection	Rival	wrk	$30	$40
Pots, cooking, copper, set of 4	West	good	$7	$12
TV b/w UHF ant	man, KTV	wrk	$25	$35
Typewriter, electric	IBM (C)	wrk	$60	$75

A list like this makes good sense because you will know exactly what items you have for sale. In most cases, if you have recorded it, you will know the make and model of the item and whether it is working or not. And you will have a price range from which to determine your final asking price. Instead of working by memory, you will have a record to refer to that has the exact information. Consider the high price as the price that you feel the item is worth to you. You can arrive at this asking price by knowing the retail price of the item and reducing its value accordingly, or you can research the item from a reliable secondhand source or guidebook. The range between the high and low asking price is your haggling range. Always hold out for your high price at first. If someone shows a definite interest in a piece, but their offer is below your low price, hold out until the offer matches or exceeds your low asking price. Be firm as to what your absolute low price will be. Don't tell your customer that you must have a certain amount to "feel good" about the deal. Keep your figures to yourself. State your high (or asking) price first, then wait for a solid bid. If you are satisfied with the offer, mark the item off your list, and sell!

Using the inventory list can serve another function. When your figures are totaled at the end of the sale, this can tell you how much you have made in sold items in relation to your entire inventory. You can put this information in terms of percentages. If you sell $600.00 out of a potential $1000.00 inventory, your end profit is sixty percent. If you have advertised in newspapers or shopping magazines, and you know what zones you have covered, then you can attribute this sixty percent profit to those zones. With future garage sales you can buy different zones and record this same percentage profit. With several sales and using experimentation by shifting your ads into different zones, you can find out which zones do better than others. You might see only a five or seven percent difference, but if this difference is consistent, you can conclude that the higher percentage zones are the ones that give you the best profit.

Also note the difference in your percentage profit between regular weekends and holiday weekends. This precise record keeping will give you a strategy every time you consider having a sale.

To tag or not to tag. That will be a question. Price tagging merchandise has advantages, but it reduces a certain amount of flexibility for the buyer and the seller. Price tags are an indication to the public that a fixed price is being asked. People are reluctant to make an offer on goods that are plainly marked for a set amount. Price tagging has been exclusive to all wholesale and retail outlets ever since we can remember. We know that supermarket produce is priced at fixed amounts, and unless it is on sale, or available with coupon purchase, the end price of the product will not be negotiable. However, a priced good will assure you that you will not pay any more or less for it than another customer. In this sense, it is fair. In the other sense you know that you will pay the listed price whether you like it or not. Priced goods also free up the seller's time. The seller will not have to debate within his high-low range, nor bicker over the price of goods.

There is a way to have the best of both worlds. You can tag it but leave the price open for discussion. This is when you add the initials OBO to the price tag. OBO stands for "Or Best Offer." It means that the figure written is the asking price but any reasonable offer will be considered. In other words, the buyer can make a bid, and the seller will work with him to come to an agreement.

The OBO designation works fine in the newspapers and shopping magazines. The seller who places this type of ad simply has to make calls, record the phone number of the bidders, and get back to the bidder with the highest offer. You see a "?" after the price figure. This means the same thing as the OBO. A "trade for?" phrase means just that. What would you like to trade of equal value for the item advertised?

When items are not plainly marked with fixed prices it is an indication that the seller knows what he wants for the item or that he is open to offers. Non-priced goods offer a more casual or relaxed atmosphere for the buyer. It tells him that the reason for the sale is not primarily the issue of getting the most money, but it is more of an invitation to chat and make an offer.

Both the tag and no-tag situation work well at garage sales. I've noticed a slightly better sales percentage with the no-tag sale. At the no-tag sale, the customer seems to linger more. Many people feel that fixed price tagging at garage sales is hypocritical and that it represents a small threat. It puts a limitation on their bargaining ability.

Chapter Eight

EASY REPAIR/MAINTENANCE & DEMONSTRATION TECHNIQUES
Broken Tasket Gaskets

It would be almost impossible to provide a complete troubleshooting guide for every product that has ever appeared on the market. The information in just the repair manuals would fill the volumes of an encyclopedia. Indeed, there are complete encyclopedia sets available that specialize in carpentry, plumbing, heating and air conditioning, electricity, engines, and other home repairs. Since the garage seller and buyer often considers electrically operated devices for sale or purchase, this chapter will attempt to introduce the reader to the basic concepts of these products and how they operate. Gasoline engines, such as those on lawnmowers and edgers, will also be mentioned. The seller and buyer will be enlightened as to what to look for when considering these items for sale and purchase. Rather than going into full technical detail on electric motors and engines, we will confine ourselves to some basic "rules of thumb" when putting these devices to the test. We will troubleshoot some other common products using some simple techniques.

Troubleshooting, the steps and devices that are used to find out why a motor or engine does not function, is very important from a buyer's standpoint, since the buyer is encouraged to troubleshoot an appliance or engine before the purchase. By the same token, the seller has a responsibility to the customer, in that he should not sell merchandise that is hopelessly damaged, unless he informs the purchaser. Whereupon a purchaser, knowing the product's condition in advance, might buy for a "parts only" reason.

We as consumers face the everyday occurrence of buying products. We take them home only to find out that sometimes they don't work at all. If it is a large purchase like a microwave oven or a home video unit, we find ourselves frustrated, put out, and sometimes very angry. Most retail-bought goods do come with some type of warranty or guarantee. So at least we are assured that the manufacturer will correct the problem by giving us a new unit, or providing us with a refund. In short, satisfaction is guaranteed. Not so, in garage sales. In garage sales, items fall under the category of "As Is" purchases. Even though the phrase "As Is" is not plainly posted at garage sales and swap meets, the message is implied. The consumer is supposed to understand the conditions under which he is purchasing. Why? Because we are dealing with used merchandise. Chances are, the warranty or guarantee on such items has long since expired. There will be no service department to assist you or hear your plea. The saying, "buyer beware" has a truthful ring to it, especially with secondhand merchandise. Be forewarned. There is a risk factor here.

It becomes a question of "does the reduced cost justify the purchase of this item, if I find out later that the repair bill will exceed the original retail price of the item?" In many cases, this is such a stark reality that you could possibly throw yourself into needless debt over an item that has been discontinued or damaged past the point of repair. The biggest problem you will face in garage and swap meet purchasing will be the probability of being "stung." Ripped off. And this is very sad. It will happen in greater or lesser amounts to different individuals, but most assuredly, it will happen in some degree to everyone. This is the chance we take: the realization of that ultimate bargain might be offset by a few other bad deals. Bad deals that have left us with a totally useless investment.

To be forewarned is to be armed against bad judgment. Or, "An ounce of prevention is worth a pound of cure."

TROUBLESHOOTING AND LIGHT REPAIR

A seller who does not offer merchandise that is reasonably functional, or meets its original operating potential, is worthless to the consumer and to himself. Every honest effort should be made to assure the customer that what he is buying works. If a full demonstration is called for, the seller should comply. It is not unreasonable for a buyer to ask a seller for a demonstration. It should be mandatory! Money carries the same value when spent in any amount. Products that do not perform are not worthy of any monetary value. A seller should not expect to take good money for non-working goods. What possible excuse could a seller have for selling broken products, especially if it is internal damage, known only to him? Don't give me that, "it's junk, anyway" routine. Once and for all, if it is junk, it belongs at the junk yard. It is not an item that merits resale. A third member (automobile rear end) that came out of a 1961 Ford Fairlane, with a broken pinion gear, a chipped ring gear, and a cracked housing is junk. It is an item that is even worthless to a junk yard! It has no place in any sale.

A seller is the quality control department of his garage or swap meet sale. The integrity of his goods is a direct reflection of his attitude toward the public. If you sell on a serious level, week after week, to hundreds of people, you will want to project an image of loyalty and integrity to all of your customers. If you do not care what your customers think of your business ethics, you will not have those customers revisit you. Soon the word will be out. And that word will be that you are careless, inconsiderate, and a cheat to the general public.

If you want to avoid this negative image and maintain your repeat business, you will make every effort to present merchandise that is workable and is no burden to the customer. If you have an item that does not work, explain this in truth to the buyer who is eager to purchase the item. If through your attempt you have failed to repair a certain item, tell the interested customer this. Tell him what you think the needed cure will cost him. Better yet, leave broken and damaged goods off of your inventory. Don't sell them until you think that they will serve at least a parts-only need. After a customer gets home with his purchase is the wrong time for him to ask, "Why doesn't it work?" He will be thinking of you, the seller, with less than fond memories.

Tighten and lubricate working parts on hardware-related merchandise. Check goods for operability. It only takes minutes and a little attention. I once witnessed a customer handling a pair of binoculars at a sale. After looking through the eye pieces, he put the binoculars down on the table and mused to himself, "Pity, it would have been nice." Then he walked away. Curious at his reaction, I stepped over to the table and held the binoculars up to my eyes. Sure enough, I saw a hairline crack in the view. This really wouldn't have discouraged me from buying the pair since they would still function, only I noticed that the asking price was a little high, considering the damage. I turned the binoculars upside down and examined the lenses. I found a wet feather stuck to some moisture on one of the lenses. I removed the feather and used the tip of my T-shirt to wipe the lenses dry. Then I thought that maybe the next customer would buy the binoculars for $20.00.

In another instance, I saw a customer take a nasty fall off of a bike because the seat was not tightened. The seat was so loose that the customer slipped backwards off of it and fell to the pavement. You can be sure that customer changed his mind about the purchase.

Many minor product problems can be diagnosed with a phone call to an expert. Shop owners are always glad to impart a little wisdom and information to a person who is eager to listen and learn.

The following examples are basic and routine troubleshooting and preventive maintenance procedures.

Vacuum cleaners that have collection bags should be emptied of any debris. If the bag is choking full, the bag will exhaust dust through its fabric pores and the suction will be reduced. Putting a new drive band on the power spindle will insure that the power brush will rotate at its maximum revolutions. Check to see that the wheels are free of thread and hair, so that they will roll easily over the carpet.

The weed trimmers, commonly called weed eaters, that use a nylon filament line have a habit of binding up, failing to feed out extra cutting line. By taking the plastic power hub off of these trimmers, you can relieve the line that is knotted around the line spool. Simply unraveling, or getting the twists out of the line, then gently rewinding it, will set it to feeding out line again. The surest way to burn out a motor on one of these weed trimmers is to lean heavily on it, forcing it into the ground, when only sweeping motions above the ground are required.

On older typewriters that have a rubber power roller underneath the frame, the condition that causes the key's failure to register type on the paper is most times grease or dirt on the roller itself. The roller needs to be completely sterile and dry — it uses friction to spin plastic cams that make the keys strike. A little alcohol can be used to clean this piece and remove the grease. If a typewriter carriage fails to return or advance (as in many of the older IBM's) chances are that a small belt inside the frame is either misaligned or broken. Some light lubricating oil on the moving parts in the typewriter assembly will produce smooth action and functioning. Typewriters must be turned on and operated at least every six months to keep them from freezing up. This is because metal collects dust and oxidizes, causing friction on parts that need to move freely.

Many times a stereo or record player will not emit sound because the speaker wire connections are loose or the contacts are dirty. The female jack and male prong contacts can be cleaned with alcohol, or the "glaze" can be removed with light-grit sandpaper.

When channel changers and volume controls on televisions and radios produce loud static noises, the probable reason is dust on the tuner device for each of these controls. On manual TV channel changers, flipping the changer knob very rapidly a dozen times or more in one direction will free up dust on the tuner. Rapidly reversing the direction of the knob for five to six turns will knock the dust particles off completely. Thus, better reception and a steady picture can be obtained. The same procedure works on radio volume knobs. If the procedure has little effect, chances are that the tuner itself is worn and will have to be replaced.

You can check the rifling or spiral grooves in a rifle barrel by removing the bolt from the action, placing a white card over the barrel hole at the bolt location, and looking through the other end of the barrel. You should see well defined spirals in the barrel, with little or no corrosion on the inside of the barrel surface. At the end of the bolt you will find a tiny thimble-shaped piece of metal that protrudes slightly out of the bolt face. This is the firing pin. The pin should be slightly rounded on its edges, with no chips or cracks on it. To check the percussion strength of the firing pin for thirty caliber rifles, you could drop an eraser-tipped pencil down the barrel, and holding the barrel upright, pull the trigger. The pencil should leap, either within or all the way out of the barrel. Always make sure that the weapon is not loaded with live ammunition — the clip or breech should be completely empty when this is done. Inspect all bolt and hammer surfaces on rifles and shotguns for thin hairline cracks in the metal. Cracks indicate fatigued metal or excessive chamber pressures. Never load World War II or older military firearms with modern standard ammunition. The modern ammunition operates at much higher chamber pressures and can damage the weapon or cause a serious injury. Standard military loads are available for these older guns, and they are much cheaper to buy.

In washing machines a common problem occurs when the tub will not rotate at all, or there is slippage and the smell of burnt rubber. This usually points to a worn or broken drive belt. It can be replaced by removing the back or front panel of the machine. The action in some washing machine cycle

Belts can be replaced in washers and dryers

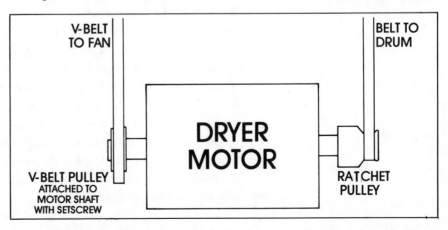

control knobs gets weak or broken and the washer will not go through some or all of the wash, rinse, and spin cycles. The control can be replaced as a unit. Some washers will refuse to drain. This might be due to a small article of clothing that has been sucked up into the pump or caught in the drain line.

When electric clothes dryers will not heat, there is probably a bad switch or a broken field in the strip-heater. They are both easily replaced.

The previous examples of repair and inspection are not meant to be "cure alls." They are common sense alternatives in an attempt to avoid the cost of expensive repair. Most general troubleshooting procedures are not applicable to all brand names and manufacturers. Take notes and create your own list of repair tips. There are numerous "fix it" books for the layman, to assist in making minor and some major repairs. Remember that many symptoms have the same cure, only the operation is different.

ELECTRICAL MOTORS

Electrically operated appliances have motors that are designed to work on household current or other sources. This current is measured in volts and usually ranges in the 110 volt range. Most household appliances function on the alternating current method. Direct current is typically used in batteries such as the automobile battery.

When plugging an appliance into a wall socket, you are providing the voltage which the motor requires to operate. Picture voltage or current as water running through a pipe. This water flow or pressure can go up or down, but nevertheless it causes the rotor or shaft of the motor to turn. Picture water flowing from a pipe over a water wheel — the wheel turns because the falling water is providing it momentum. If there is a break in the water line, the force weakens or no longer exists and the wheel will not turn.

A common electrical break in many appliances will be found in the supply cord; this is the cord that plugs into the wall socket. Cords are often pulled, yanked, and twisted — thus breaking the small wires within. This happens frequently at the plug position. A simple cure is to cut off the old plug and replace it with a new universal plug which can be purchased at a hardware store. Or the cord can become disconnected at the motor source. Most appliances have some way of removing a backing plate or cover to allow inspection of the inner workings. Sometimes you can reconnect this wire at the motor source by tightening the small screw plate that holds the wire to the lead. Other times it is a solder connection that has come loose, which requires you to resolder the joint.

Possible wire breaks in an appliance

If the cord is good and the source of electricity is sufficient to run the appliance but the appliance still will not operate, there are a few things to look for. If the appliance is plugged in, and immediately your household circuit breaker trips, it is an indication that the appliance has a direct short, or short to ground, in its windings. A short circuit is a damaging connection between two points in a circuit in the motor itself. The result is an excessive flow of current. This is an example of a motor with a direct short.

If an appliance is plugged in and it smokes from within the motor area but still operates, it means that it is overheating, causing the lacquer on the internal winding to burn. It could also be wire insulation that is burning. In this condition, the appliance will not last long.

If an appliance is plugged in and its rotor shaft spins very slowly or below normal revolutions, it is probably due to a worn rotor and brushes or electromagnetic pickups. This condition will cause a high resistance and overheat the windings. A bearing surface that is dry of lubrication could also cause this condition since it would put an additional load on the motor.

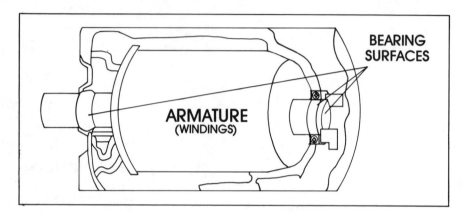

Bearing surfaces in an electric motor

What about a motor that turns on and then shuts off? As explained before, a bad supply cord with a break in the wires would do this especially when the wire was jiggled or moved. If it is not the supply cord it might be that the motor has a built-in safety feature to guard against overheating. Many small appliances have thermal protection switches. That means that if they get too hot or suffer excessive current, they will shut off automatically. These protection devices are overload switches. When they detect abnormal levels of heat or current they will open the circuit to halt the flow of current. In more expensive appliances like garage door openers, a reset switch is provided to restart the device — this is common in computers too. In the smaller handheld electric appliances like hair dryers, the switch is a small piece of bi-metal that serves as the overload device. The bi-metal will expand when it senses severe heat, thereby opening up the circuit and shutting down the appliance. When the bi-metal cools down it closes the circuit and the appliance can be turned on again.

Most motors have internal impellers or fans that are affixed to the main rotor in some way, or operate separately. If these fan blades are broken or stuck they cannot cool the motor. If they cannot cool the motor this will activate the thermal protection switch. That is why you will see little windows, screens, or vents in appliances. These vents let cool air into the fan area, where it is flushed over the motor to keep it cool. The air can be taken in at one point and exhausted out through some other port. If these vents are clogged with debris it can overheat the motor of the appliance. Thus, a motor will turn on and cut off.

Many times you can see through these vents or remove a cover to see the motor windings inside. Normal windings are shiny and copper colored. Black windings and a sooty or carbon smell indicate a problem.

Any appliance that shows any of these previous symptoms, except for clogged vents, is probably not a wise purchase. Electric motors that emit a steady hum when they attain full revolutions are basically sound and in good working order. A seller should be mindful if any of his appliances show these symptoms. These appliances are questionable, and should be excluded from the sale. Or the customer should be told about their condition before a purchase is made.

If you are an expert in the field of electronics you could further pinpoint malfunctions with meters that register volts, ohms, and amps. Motors carry amp ratings and can be checked for resistance and other factors that determine optimum performance. This knowledge would come in handy when checking out larger and more expensive electrical motors.

The grim realities when faced with small appliances, or even ones like window air conditioning units, is that they are more expensive to repair than to replace. Repair technicians require a flat rate, or charge by the hour just to troubleshoot an appliance. This is discounting parts and labor to repair it.

It seems that the only reason that appliances are assembled with screws, nuts, and bolts is so the warranty departments can take them apart to repair the manufacturers' flaws. We cannot, as general consumers, afford the expense in parts and labor to bring these products back to life. Once they are broken and worn there is little we can do to remedy the problem. Is it any wonder so many people are taking courses and collecting books on home repair? Nowadays, it is not uncommon for us to pay a $50.00 service contract along with a $200.00 item so we may be protected against major breakdowns. And the service contract is only good for the first year of ownership, and it is ironic that our products start breaking down at the two year mark.

SMALL GASOLINE ENGINES

There is definitely something we can do, as consumers, to repair and maintain our small gasoline engines. These engines are designed to be disassembled, repaired, and rebuilt. Even the ordinary lawnmower engine is easily serviced and maintained. They can provide as much as a dozen years of constant use if they are properly serviced. Broken or worn parts can be replaced.

We will confine ourselves to the four cycle engines that are used on lawnmowers and edgers. Typical brand names include: Briggs and Stratton, McCullough, Tecumseh, and Clayton. Even Honda makes a small engine for lawnmowers, but it is Briggs and Stratton that is the most widely used.

Two cycle engines, those commonly used on chain saws and leaf blowers, are a little different in design than the four cycle types. Two cycle engines operate at much faster RPMs. They have reeds instead of valves to meter the amount of fuel that enters the cylinder. Sometimes they require a mix of oil to be added to the gasoline — this helps with internal lubrication. These engines are smaller, lighter in weight, louder, and have a notorious reputation for being more temperamental than their four cycle counterparts. Many outboard motorboat engines are of the two cycle design.

Several things can go wrong with a standard four cycle engine that will not allow it to run properly, or at all. For simplicity, we will refer to these different problem areas as the air, fuel, spark (electricity), and compression systems.

Air is needed to mix with raw liquid fuel in order to ignite the mixture. A carburetor is used to determine the amount of air/fuel that will enter into the cylinder for the purpose of combustion. The carburetor also turns the air and fuel into a fine mist or spray so it burns more easily. Air has oxygen in it, and oxygen is required to cause fire. In other words, fuel from the tank and air from the atmosphere meet in the carburetor, where it is turned into a spray, then drawn into the engine by the downward suction of the piston.

The air has to be clean and plentiful. On small four cycle gasoline engines there is an air cleaner device that bolts to the top of the carburetor. It is a small metal case. Inside this case is a sponge that filters the dirt out of the air that goes into the carburetor. This small sponge should be cleaned regularly with warm soapy water, then completely dried and placed back into the metal air cleaner case. If the sponge is allowed to become caked with grease and grass particles, the engine will suffocate from lack of air and refuse to run properly.

Fuel is required as the source of ignition or fire. Fuel is sucked up from the small fuel tank and enters into the carburetor, where it mixes with air. It is then drawn into the combustion chamber where it is compressed and ignited. After it ignites it expands rapidly, shoving the piston down to complete a power stroke. Without uncontaminated fuel the engine will not run.

If the carburetor is loose where it joins to the engine block, it will allow too much air into the cylinder (a lean condition), and the engine will run unsteadily. Two bolts hold the carburetor (with gasket) against the block. They should be tightened routinely, since these engines run with a lot of vibration.

Pulling out the choke lever or plunger on the carburetor allows a rich mixture of fuel to be used by the engine for cold starting. In a few minutes, the choke should be pushed back in to allow for normal running. If the choke is left out in the rich position, a warm engine will sputter and die.

There are two adjustable screws on the carburetor: one for idle speed and one for fuel mixture. If the engine is running the mixture screw should be adjusted first. Turning this screw either in or out, in small increments, will determine its smoothest running position. If the engine is not running, an initial adjustment can be made to begin a starting point. Turn the mixture screw in (clockwise), until it bottoms out. Then turn it in the opposite direction (out), one and one-half turns. At this position the engine should start and further fine tuning can be performed.

The idle speed screw can then be set by turning it in (clockwise) to increase engine speed, or out (counterclockwise) to decrease it.

Spark is required to ignite the air/fuel mixture when it enters the combustion chamber. A small magneto located near the flywheel provides spark, or voltage to the spark plug via the ignition points and condenser. The spark plug screws into the head at the top of the engine. By taking the spark plug wire off of the plug and holding it close to a bare metal surface of the engine block, you can pull the pull rope and watch for a spark to jump from the wire to the block. The spark will be a quick burst of blue-white electricity. If a spark is seen this means that the ignition is working properly.

If no spark is seen it means that the problem will lie in the ignition points and/or condenser. The ignition points can be reached by removing the metal engine cowl, usually three or four bolts. By removing the centrifugal hub for the pull start and the flywheel, you can gain access to the points and condenser. They will be inside a small circular metal case. You can buy a points and condenser kit for around ten dollars and install them yourself. They will come with very simple installation instructions and they will not take more than thirty minutes to install. Point surfaces often burn. Condensers often short out. This is a very common cause for a no-start situation. When you replace the points and condenser, along with the spark plug, it is called a tune-up.

Another electronic culprit that often fails is the spark plug itself, since it endures an enormous amount of pressure and heat. Unscrewing the plug from the top of the engine (the head) will let you examine it. The small metal nipple underneath the "L" shaped rod is the electrode. The electrode should have the shape of a small cylinder with clean sharp edges. The normal coloration for it is a crusty white/brown. It if is black, it is an indication that the choke has been left out, or that the fuel mixture screw has been turned out too far. If the electrode is severely rounded or reduced in size, it means that it is worn and should be replaced. Plugs also have a gap. That gap is the distance between the "L" shaped arm and the top of the electrode. This distance is measured in thousandths of an inch — usually expressed .035 or .045. You make this adjustment with a "feeler gauge." By tapping the "L" gently, you can close the gap. Prying it open will increase the gap.

Assuming that all of these functions are in order, the air, fuel, and spark, there is another reason why the engine may fail to start. There could be a compression problem. Inside the engine is a cylinder. In the cylinder there is a piston that rides up and down this sleeve. It is the piston's job to compress the air/fuel mixture. Two valves are required to monitor the intake and exhaust of the engine. The intake valve opens to allow fuel to enter, the exhaust valve opens to allow burned exhaust gases to escape.

A simple way to check for compression is to remove the spark plug, place your thumb over the hole, and pull the pull rope. You should feel a blast of air under your thumb each time the piston rises to the top — in this case, several strong puffs or blasts. If you feel no strong air blasts at all, there is no doubt that an engine part is broken. The broken internal part will be either the piston, a piston ring (this encircles the piston to make it fit snugly in the cylinder), a broken connecting rod (this holds the piston in place), or it may be a burned exhaust valve. The only other exception to this would be a blown head gasket. This cardboard or metal gasket fits between the head and the engine block to form a tight seal. If an engine runs with a blown head gasket it will sometimes spit oil, and always make a constant racket-like hiss.

The side cover of the engine can be removed to gain access to these internal parts. These parts are not as expensive as you would believe. Twenty dollars might buy you the needed part. That is a far cry from the price of a new engine. Several repair manuals are available to the customer who wishes to fix his own engine. If he has several gasoline-operated gardening tools, he could perform his own periodic tune-ups, oil changes, and other maintenance services.

The pull ropes often break on lawnmowers. It is simple to fix them. By removing the engine cowl and looking on the inside of the cowl, you will see a circular winding mechanism. You can pull this out of the cowl, retrieve the broken rope, rewind the mechanism (it is spring loaded) and the rope, and feed it back up through the cowl hole. You can then thread the rope through the pull handle and knot it, to keep it from passing through the handle opening. There are small ball bearings on the inside of the winding mechanism —

be certain not to lose them if the mechanism comes apart in two halves. The ball bearings must be replaced back into the slots that are provided for them.

If a power mower does not cut grass efficiently it is because the riding height adjustment is too high, or the blade underneath needs to be sharpened. In the latter case, a lawnmower shop will sharpen a blade for around eight to ten dollars.

Rear or side bag grass catchers are a nice convenience on a lawnmower. They negate the need to rake the lawn since they collect the cuttings. If a buyer finds a lawnmower that he likes but it has no grass catcher, a universal bag and assembly kit can be purchased from a lawnmower shop. These kits come with adapters and hardware along with an instruction booklet. You might need a power drill to drill a few holes into the lawnmower grass pan.

Edger engines are virtually the same as the lawnmower variety. On an edger, the blade will be smaller but it has to be sharpened like the lawnmower blade. An edger also has an additional clutch control that engages a drive to operate the function of the cutting blade. Blade angle and height adjustments can be made on most popular edgers.

On the upright engine models, the oil drain plug is at the bottom of the engine block. It can be removed with a crescent wrench or an open end wrench. On the side-mount type engines, the drain plug is commonly found underneath the grass pan of the lawnmower and can be removed in the same manner as the upright. The oil pans hold one to two quarts of regular engine oil. Thirty weight detergent type oil is recommended. Regular gasoline is used in these small motors. High test fuel can burn the valves and cause them to overheat.

These small engines are also found on rotor-tillers, self-propelled and tractor lawnmowers, portable electric generators, and older style mini bikes and go-karts. If they are four cycle engines, the repair procedures will be the same.

Chapter Nine

SALESMANSHIP AND COURTESY

Bend with the Forest Trees or Break

Salesmanship goes hand in hand with courtesy. The talent does not precede the virtue, nor does the virtue, courtesy, have priority over the talent, salesmanship. The two factors should be considered the whole of the package. For without one, the other is one dimensional, without purpose or direction. Strong salesmanship coupled with attentive courtesy is an unbeatable combination.

Salesmanship is the driving force or need to sell oneself and one's product. The product itself has little value if the vehicle for selling it is not in order. Salespersons must take a great deal of confidence and pride in themselves. The world is full of discouragement and rejection. The resourceful salesperson must rise above minor defeats and setbacks, learn from past errors, and devise new campaigns to adjust to the ever changing demands of the consumer. The salesperson must keep tabs on fads and trends, and be willing to anticipate market changes. The salesperson must be thoroughly familiar with his/her product, with enough knowledge to explain its merits and advantages over competitive alternatives. A salesperson's attitude must be energetic, creative, and positive, with room left over in the makeup for flexibility and the wish to learn. With the need to have all of these attributes, and still get the job done, it is truly sad sometimes how much the salesperson is misunderstood.

Therefore, a salesperson must show signs of courtesy. Courtesy is patience and a willingness to listen to others. It is a virtue that must cool the heads of the flamboyant. Courtesy allows for grace and the proper timing when confronted with overwhelming odds. It is an emphatic bridge between two human beings amid the din of business and responsibility. It is a soft gleam on a sharp cutting edge. It is a balm of finesse that soothes the frantic rush of everyday life. A great salesperson with courtesy not only cares for himself, but others and their needs. A great salesperson offers to others something of value that he truly believes in himself.

THE BLOCK SALE PHENOMENON

One of the greatest examples of salesmanship and courtesy that I have ever seen has been demonstrated by our own block sale sponsors. I think that Bill Guzzardo and his associate, Reita Huddleston, have set a major precedent in garage sale history, if there is such a thing. I don't rightly know where the idea of block sales originated from. Since my first experience with them was from Bill, I tend to think that he started the affair, some years back. All I know is that I have never seen such a campaign launched with such success, in such a short time. I think that Bill has that midas touch, except that aside from profits, he has reached out and turned everyone he's touched into a friend. Since he is a realtor, I can see how advantageous it is for him to come up with such an idea. Since his success as a realtor relies heavily on personal contacts, he couldn't have picked a better avenue than that of becoming our neighborhood sponsor. As a result of his efforts he has managed to raise a platform of friendship within the neighborhood. He has everyone talking about him, in all good senses of the term. And he has also escalated his own realty business into a much higher profit bracket.

I don't know how popular block sales are with the rest of the nation. I don't think that they are unique to just our community. Certainly, in the last three years they have ignited interest within our neighborhood. When the campaign comes up every six months or so, we see more and more sale participants and outside buyers. I believe that if the general public becomes aware of the fun and advantages of block sales, the practice will ultimately sweep the nation!

Let's examine how and what Bill does to bring thousands of dollars into his immediate neighborhood. It starts when Bill knows that it's time to "rally" the neighborhood. Bill feels this urge about every six months, May and October, so he usually has two events each year. The first thing he does is to pass out invitation flyers to every house in the neighborhood. These flyers are passed out at least a month in advance. He prints the flyers up to inform the residents of a block sale, including the day of the event and the time. He includes his phone number on the flyer with the request that all interested parties contact him, with their name, phone number, and address. Residents call him back and inform him of their commitment to "join in." After Bill has received his responses, which takes about a week's time, he makes a tentative list of the sale houses, and their locations. He transfers these sale houses to a special aerial map, not a photograph, but an overhead diagram of the entire neighborhood, with the streets and houses shown in exact scale and relation to each other. Referring to his list, he then blacks out the sale houses with a felt pen. This way he records all participants, not only by address, but by a convenient visual aid that assists buyers in finding the sale houses. This also helps the buyer know where the "cluster sales" are. It is common to see ten blacked-out houses in a row. This signifies a "hot" area. A buyer has only to park his car in the vicinity and visit many sales at once.

During the next couple of weeks Bill records the late responses and fits them into his map accordingly. He sends out a final notice flyer to confirm the number of sellers that he will be providing for. He also begins to assemble his store-bought garage sale signs by stapling the signs onto four foot stakes that he has bought at the lumber yard.

A week before the actual sale, Bill takes out ad space in the shopping magazines and the newspapers. It is also at this time that he visits all of the sale houses and gives the sellers copies of the map. Additional maps are given to the sellers so that they can hand out extras to the customers. The customers will use the maps during the entire time that they are at the block sale. The repeat customers have come to expect the map, knowing that it is a permanent part of the function.

A day before the sale, on Friday, Bill and Reita tape five eight foot banners over all entrances of the housing tract. Reita does the letter and design work on the banners after they have been taped to the walls. She uses different colors to attract attention, making sure that her lettering and arrows are large enough to be seen from the street.

On the day of the sale, very early in the morning, Bill and Reita distribute all of the garage sale signs to the participating sellers. Bill uses over a hundred signs, making sure that every house gets one, sometimes two, and places the remaining signs at other locations throughout the surrounding neighborhood. After Bill is sure that the sale is properly set up, he dashes off and returns with a dozen cartons of donuts to pass around to the sleepy-eyed sellers. This is enough to feed the fifty to seventy homes that are participating, out of the total 580. He only stipulates that the homes provide their own coffee.

When the sale gets in full swing, a phenomenon occurs. Homes that had not signed up for participation are suddenly caught up in the fever. They begin a frantic hustle to set up display tables, organize goods, and do their best to look just like the other sellers — relaxed and ready for the crowds. So with this additional ten to fifteen homes, who are suddenly asking where their maps and signs are, Bill finds himself very busy at the last minute attending to the late starters.

The rush comes. At around 9:00 AM the day of the sale, a normal resident would swear that a crowd at a local football stadium has just gotten lost and ended up in the neighborhood. This is the foot traffic. The car traffic is so intense that the local police department, while writing out parking tickets, helps with the directions, and gets caught up in the sale themselves.

Some of the sellers are specialized. Buyers frequently ask where the "computer man" is, or where the "furniture lady" is located. As the sale progresses buyers stop each other for directions or tips on the choice sale houses. Even the sellers link up with each other. The computer man always sends customers to the office supplies man. The sports equipment man knows who has the most bicycles in the sale, besides himself. And so it goes.

Before the neighborhood has realized that it has had a sale, the sale is over. Then Bill and Reita take down all of the banners and retrieve their signs. Sellers wearily clear off their lawns and driveways. As the sun sets, there can be heard the muffled shuffling of paper money and the clinking of coins, in the once again quiet neighborhood.

Our neighborhood can always proclaim that we are richer for knowing Bill and Reita. This is true in both senses, since we all know that the entire production is paid for by them. Not one house has to buy anything, or is ever asked to contribute. This is something that Bill and Reita do for the neighborhood. They absorb the cost of the ads, the signs, the maps, flyers, notices, and refreshments, not to mention contributing their time and labor to the project. What do they get in return?

Our support and devotion.

If we want to sell a house, they are the first to be notified. If we know of someone who wants to sell a house, they are the first to be notified. Virtually any way that we can show our appreciation to them, we will. After all, they have shown us how a neighborhood can function as a unit and get things done. They've brought us all together under a familiar envelope. It goes without saying that we all know each other now. We protect each others property. We are mindful of our neighbors' children. It has been revealed to us that cooperation is the key that opens many locked doors.

For people who are interested in becoming block sale sponsors, here is a checklist (Bill's formula) for starting the event.

THINGS TO DO

□ The opening notice. One month before sale. This is a flyer that states your intention to run a block sale — the time and date of the sale and your intention to advertise. Include your phone number so you can be reached for verification.

□ Final notice, two weeks before sale. This is a reminder that you send to verified sale houses with mention that the sale day is approaching. Ask if they will be ready. Are they collecting and preparing sale items? Do they wish to withdraw?

□ Maps. These are sent out one week before the sale. All sale houses are accounted for and included on this schematic. The maps are distributed to sale houses at this time along with extra copies for customers. Ads are placed with the newspapers and shopping magazines at this time. Construction of sale signs begins.

□ Banners and signs go up. One day before sale, or very early morning of sale day. Late-start houses are found and asked if they want assistance.

□ Refreshments (optional).

□ End of sales. Remove all signs and banners from neighborhood.

Becoming a block sale sponsor is not for everyone. It does cost money, time, and labor to produce one. If you don't have the funds to start one, you can send out a pre-flyer that asks for a small contribution from all interested parties. With a small treasury of funds, the ads, signs, and banners can be easily purchased or made. Or the responsibilities can be delegated to three or four individuals. A computer owner might volunteer to produce the flyers. Someone else could create the signs. Still another could chip in for the newspaper and shopping magazine ads. Whatever means used to produce the sale are worth the effort.

NEW NEIGHBORS AND FRIENDS

If there was ever a reason for a community to come together, the block sale is no finer example. City council meetings, neighborhood watch programs, and earthquake disaster seminars are great opportunities for people to come together. But somehow, these meetings still have an impersonal flavor to them, and regardless of how many times we attend them, we still don't meet enough local neighbors who share our wider interests. Garage and swap meet sales afford us the chance and time to really get to know each other. The blessing comes when you find someone with an occupation that you admire, or selling a product that you badly need. If you have something that he likes, a trade or swap is a wonderful fringe benefit.

A seller who meets another seller he likes will drop his protective barriers. He will open up and thrive on the discussion of ideas and deals. I know, because I saved $800.00 on a computer by dealing with a seller who knew the business and owned a small operation. Here is how it happened. In the midst of tending one of my own sales during a block sale event, I was questioned by a young man about an old computer relic that was standing off in the back of my garage. I only remarked to him that it was just that, an old CPM relic that did not work. I said that I wished that I had one of the newer IBM clones — a computer with a more advanced operating system because I was becoming tired of using a typewriter. I wanted something that I could truly edit with, like a word processor. The young man casually remarked that his father's garage was packed with such computers and that they were being sold at that very moment, not two streets away.

This was how I met the computer man. Upon hearing this I turned my sale over to my sister and followed the young man home. There I met his father, Don McFarland, who indeed had turned his garage into a computer assembly plant and service center. Several models were displayed on tables in his driveway. Since I knew little or nothing about these strange machines, I confronted Don and asked him to rescue me from my child-like ignorance. It was evident that I was in the hands of an expert — notice that I didn't say at his mercy. With all of the honesty that I could muster I simply said, "I want one of those. Could you please help me? The kids nowadays know more about them than I do." He understood perfectly. He began to explain to me everything that I wanted to know about those machines. As though he was narrating a story from a child's book, he taught me the very basic fundamentals and theories behind computers and operating systems. After an hour, I was hopelessly hooked and bedazzled by this man's sincerity and knowledge. This computer thing was more fascinating than I ever imagined. I felt that I was an expert already, so I decided to take the plunge. He explained to me that "oversell" in the computer industry was a common practice, and that the buyer was usually the one who suffered in the deal. So he said that he would design for me a custom package that would give me not any less, or any more, than what I needed for my application. I told him exactly what I wanted it for, which was to put words on paper, and maybe play a few of the games that I had heard so much about.

He said that a color card was necessary because I had the desire to play games. So that was a simple matter and he would install that. He said that a color monitor was needed so that I could actually see the colors. He asked me how much writing I did. I said a great deal. So a hard disk drive would have to be installed, not a whopper, but a modest one. If I reached a point where I filled the present hard disk, he would exchange it for a larger one at no cost in labor. He said that the computer itself could be of the XT variety since I did not need to work with elaborate or exotic programs. Though he said that the XT was slower, it would not function any slower than my ability to think. This sounded reasonable. I didn't want a computer that would out-think me, or race pell-mell ahead into an unlimited threshold. Don assured me that the computer that he would assemble for me would be "user friendly," and that after awhile the two of us, the computer and me, would be "shaking hands."

The author's $600.00 pearl

Two days later I shook hands with my new XT computer. The computer, keyboard, brand new CTX color monitor, two operating manuals, new floppies, dozens of software programs, a box of fanfold paper, and all the other modifications that were performed at my request, cost me $600.00. This was such a substantial savings that I couldn't believe my ears. He told me that he had passed some of his savings on the equipment off onto me — his wholesale benefits. Not to mention that I was a preferred customer and that I had immediate service and hot-line priority. He said that he would back the purchase as long as I owned it, and that it would never depreciate in value. This was so I could later up-trade it for a larger model if I so desired.

His genuine need to please me prompted me to remit in some way. I was a newspaper reporter, so the only thing that I had to offer him was a lengthy writeup in my paper. This would give him some exposure and credit for a job well done. I did this for him, and he was quite pleased with the attention. I also found another person like myself who wanted a system. She had been led on a merry ride with several computer dealers who had told her that she must have this, and that she shouldn't do without that. It rang a familiar bell. I immediately thought of Don as the best prospect to unravel her doubts. It was two weeks later when she took possession of the model that was just right for her. It came from Don, with all of the blessings, guarantees, and options that had been given to me. The result was a very happy lady, an appreciative computer dealer, and as for myself, the knowledge that I had been of some help to someone.

This manner of inside trading catches on like wildfire. Like a smile it is contagious. It is something akin to the good neighbor policy, something that many of us have forgotten, or have swept under the rug. You suddenly find yourself referred to someone else, they in turn have someone who wants to talk to you, and before you know it you've made more profitable contacts in one year than you have in ten.

Since my encounter with Don a year ago, his business has taken off to such heights that he is now cutting back on production and commitments. He maintains his service responsibility, just as he had promised, but he is so inundated at times he has little time for his family. So he has to take time off. His idea of leisure is to pack up the family, load the van with computer hardware, and set up at the Computer Swap Meet. Don relates that he has no time to move into his own office or shop. He's too busy filling orders at the swap meet!

It goes something like, "You can please half of the people half of the time, some of the people some of the time, but you can't please all of the people all of the time." Don believes that you can *try* to please all of the people all of the time.

Chapter Ten

PROBLEM ITEMS AND DISSATISFACTION
The Better to Eat You With!

"Don't sell the steak; sell the sizzle" is a popular salesman's slogan. It has been used many times to hype a product. There are as many tricks in salesmanship as there are honest virtues. Sometimes, we as consumers are compelled to buy something from an emotional rush that we get. We receive these signals through subliminal advertising or outright deception. The fact remains: we end up with a product and wonder why we bought it. Or worse, how we spent good money for something and got gypped in the deal. Likewise, the seller can inadvertently make a permanent enemy through a mistake in merchandising or use of pressure or hard sell tactics.

We will examine what the buyer should know when confronting questionable merchandise, and where the seller should be cautious in releasing goods to the public. There will be a slightly greater emphasis on the part of the seller, in terms of products to avoid. If the seller is aware of problem areas and avoids them, it leaves a more risk-free path for the buyer. So that it does, begin first with the seller and what he is offering the public. The seller who does not gamble protects his buyer from disappointment. For the FTC (Federal Trade Commission) or the Better Business Bureau will not intervene in a case of misrepresentation or fraud in a garage sale dispute. Even a small claims court would be unlikely to review disposition in a dispute over an "As Is" purchase in a garage sale. An exception might be a professional swap meet vendor who represents a company and sells their products.

HEADACHE MERCHANDISE

Our examination will begin with the garage sale seller. The seller will save money and embarrassment by knowing which items to avoid. Since electrical motors and gasoline engines have been mentioned, some other items will be noted, along with the reasons why they are potential troublemakers. It is strongly recommended that a seller who wants to avoid legal altercations post a sign, plainly for all to see, amongst his goods. The sign should read: "Notice, all purchases are AS IS. No returns."

Baby toys just don't do well at garage sales. One of the primary reasons is that everything associated with a newborn baby is clean, innocent, and fresh. Clean in the sense that people are very hygiene conscious when buying items for a baby. Brand new baby toys that are found in department stores are sterilized and securely packaged to guard against germs and bacteria. These new packaged toys have not been exposed to the atmosphere nor to other babies' mouths. Mothers are reluctant to purchase secondhand baby toys. New baby toys are not expensive, so there is really no need to sell them secondhand. One of the worst examples of seller etiquette would be the display of a used pacifier for sale. This would also apply to rattles and other teething products. There seems to be a more liberal view with children's toys, though, because we assume that children have had their necessary shots and are more resilient to infection. Remember, use caution with infant toys.

Games are the biggest time drainer in a garage sale. They demand the lowest prices and produce the most frustration. Board games are the leading culprits. These secondhand games are rarely complete, and if they are minus just one piece, many times it makes the game unusable. This applies to the little plastic tokens, cards, spinning wheels, and all manner of gear that is required to play them. A game with the box seal broken is a terrible gamble. The first thing missing is the directions. Thereafter any part could be missing and who would know what it was? Also, children delight in dismantling games right there on the sale site. When the Monopoly money begins to blow like snow over your yard, you will know what I mean. Even if your games are complete, and you know for a fact that they are complete, tape them shut. If you don't you will wonder where all those pretty little playing pieces went in the hustle.

This goes double for a previously opened jigsaw puzzle. Especially the kind that are 1500 pieces or more strong. A used jigsaw puzzle that has a questionable population inside is junk! Of course, they do make good kindling to start fires.

Hand guns. Not at a garage sale. I will sell a handgun through a more personal and legitimate channel. I'll sell a hand gun to another NRA member that I know, and in the privacy of my home. Not on the street to a stranger. I am even beginning to exclude toy guns and rifles from my sale, for personal reasons. I have sold toy guns in the past, but I have done some serious thinking along these lines, and I do not want to project the wrong image to children. That's why B.B. and pellet guns are off my list. A true gun is a tool to be used as such. A B.B. or pellet gun breeds mischief because it is an imitation, and too frequently used within city limits.

While we're at it, switchblade knives, martial arts weapons, and brass knuckles would find no place in my sale. City laws and ordinances are the reason. Firecrackers and other pyrotechnic devices are also a potential hazard to the public.

Automobiles. Cars and trucks sold as a stand-alone item in shopping magazines or newspapers are a good bet. In garage sales, and without preparation, they can present problems. In the State of California, for example, a smog certificate is required on vehicles every time there is a change of ownership. This means that the smog control hardware attached to the vehicle must be present and in perfect working order. The vehicle must be currently registered. If it is not, the Department of Motor Vehicles will want to know why. If it hasn't been registered, a certificate of non-operation must be filled out to prove that the vehicle has not been used on the streets with expired registration. Even if the vehicle is in good running condition and has current registration, it can still fail a smog check. This can bring the buyer back to the seller in a fit of desperation, wanting to know why the vehicle has failed.

Has the vehicle been modified by the use of another component installed on the engine? Is the engine so worn that this is the reason it fails a smog test? Must the vehicle have a major tune up before it is sold, to pass the inspection?

The Department of Motor Vehicles requires current proof of ownership. Does your name appear on the pink slip? Where is the pink slip? You must have it to release interest in the vehicle. Has the past record of the vehicle been cleared of all equipment and parking violations? If not, the potential buyer could end up with a vehicle with numerous fines imposed against it. Discounting the condition of the vehicle, remember that all of the paperwork must be completed to the satisfaction of the Department of Motor Vehicles before the sale is made!

Computer software. When selling software (floppy disks with programs on them), are you selling the original programs complete with the directions? If you are selling pirated copies, where are the directions required to access the programs? It is against the law to make multiple copies of a software package that is copyright protected. If you sell copied software programs, how can you guarantee them?

Record albums. Used phonograph albums that have been stored for some time are rather an "iffy" purchase. They are easily scratched if they are not properly covered. Left in the sunshine without a cover, they easily warp, distorting the record, which can damage phonograph needles. Before selling records and albums make sure that they are clean and not physically damaged.

Audio tapes. Four and eight track audio tapes were the rage at one time. They were used in automotive tape decks and household units. They have been nearly phased out of the market completely. The standard audio cassette has taken the place of these older tapes, and are now the popular products to produce sound recordings. Unless the buyer is a collector of old four and eight track tapes, I would not include them in the sale.

CPM computer hardware. CPM computers were the nation's operating standard years ago. Like four and eight track tapes, they have been gradually phased out of the market place. They have a limited memory size, usually 64K, are slow in operating parameters, and require the 8 inch floppy disk in most cases. Parts for the floor-mount models are becoming increasingly difficult to find. The software can only be acquired through mail order, or through some of the local user groups. Most computer technicians do not have the facilities or desire to repair these units. In fact most of the present day technicians do not even know what CPM is. The trade-in value on these units is almost nil, and their value is continuing to decline at an alarming rate.

Old CPM operating system

CPM computers require terminals instead of monitors. Terminals have different operating parameters than monitors. Many CPM computers are multi-users which require additional terminals for networking capabilities. Remember that terminals and monitors are component hardware. They are designed to work in conjunction with a CPU, or brain, which is the computer itself.

Floor mount CPM and monitor

The popular computers sold today are of IBM and MacIntosh design. Parts and software programs are readily available for these computers. They can be upgraded with the addition of optional components, with many of the add-on parts easily installed by the owner. The computer industry is an ever-changing and progressive market. New innovations are continually being introduced to the consumer. Design and development trends are happening so fast that the potential customer in search of a computer would be wise to research the popular publications that keep current information on all products new and used. One such publication is *Personal Computing*, published by Hayden/VNU publications.

Auto parts. General auto parts, as a rule, are commonly found in garage and swap meet sales. There are some parts that require bench testing before they should be purchased. These would include starters, generators, alternators, regulators, carburetors, and batteries. Automobile electrical components present a problem since they are difficult to diagnose on the spot without the proper instruments to check their operability. In fact, most auto parts stores refuse to refund money on electrical items since so many things can go wrong with them during installation. Therefore, their policy is to swap the component for a similar make and design, or to offer another make and design equal in value and performance to the original. For instance, batteries should be fully charged, checked with a hydrometer, then put under a load test to determine their strength and condition. Starters need to be checked for amperage draw which determines the condition of the armature and inner workings. Alternators must be bench-tested for voltage output, which is about 14.2 volts maximum.

Several auto parts stores offer a free check service on these components. They have the machines and instruments to determine the reliability of electrical items. Auto service centers also have these machines, but they might charge a slight fee in checking them.

Transmissions, engines, and carburetors. Carburetors are extremely difficult to diagnose. They have many internal parts: check-balls, springs, valves, and diaphragms. A carburetor that has been sitting for a long time is susceptible to dust, moisture, and weathering. The weathering on the inside is of greater concern; many carburetors have rubber diaphragms that, with age, crack and lose their ability to seal. Air bleeds and needle valve seats can become clogged with the smallest of particles. There is no way to check out a carburetor other than installing it on a vehicle, or rebuilding it altogether.

The same applies to transmissions. They have a great many internal parts and must be disassembled for inspection, or actually road tested. An easy visual inspection of a transmission would be the examination of its fluid. Fluid that is dark brown or black, accompanied by a burnt odor, is evidence of an overheated or poorly kept transmission. The internal bands and clutches can also be worn.

Engines. Automobile engines are very risky business when offered for sale. The engine is the heart of the car, and no one can really be sure that an engine is functional unless a costly tear-down is performed, or it is road tested. An engine could be damaged internally beyond reasonable repair. Remanufactured heads and short blocks, as they are called, are okay if some kind of a warranty is provided with them. It is rare to even see these larger engines and parts for sale at swap meets.

Pets. Domesticated animals and pets can be a real problem for the seller. Selling any pet to a child, at a garage sale or swap meet, almost guarantees that the creature will be returned. Your chances are better if you are selling to an adult, but there is the distinct possibility that the pet will die soon after the sale. Many pets, like turtles, fish, and even some birds, are sensitive to changes in environment. Animals experience trauma much like people, and when separated from loving owners develop behavioral problems. There may also be underlying reasons for selling a pet — viciousness, cost and upkeep, or indifference to the animal.

The sale of many exotic-type animals and most wild animals is prohibited by law. In many cases these animals require special permits to be kept in city limits. This is to guard against infectious diseases like rabies.

Likewise, pet toys and chew bones are not recommended for resale. For instance, dog saliva carries bacteria and germs, even some diseases, that can be transmitted through these types of products.

Food and fruit. Some of the most stringent laws in the country are levied against persons who openly sell food without the proper permits and licenses. Regardless of good intentions or a loving heart, absolutely, DO NOT SELL FOOD OR PRODUCE AT GARAGE SALES. Licensed vendors at swap meets are equipped to do this. You are not. Don't even consider selling fruit from your trees to the public. In a case of botulism you could be sued for a considerable amount. It is doubtful that you could prove innocence or ignorance of the law. I would not even mess with canned goods — the penalties are too high to risk it. Packaged candies could be even worse. Someone could claim that you deliberately injected a substance into the packaging. Even though you believe that it would be impossible to convict you for such a slight, why expend the time and money in court finding this out?

A licensed food vendor

Acceptable refreshments would be takeout food, ice water, or maybe some lemonade. And even this falls into a "gray area." Use sound judgment when offering refreshments or snacks to the public. People are extremely sensitive when it comes to something that is ingested. This is why Halloween is becoming more and more unpopular.

Sports equipment. There is no doubt that sports equipment is one of the best overall sellers in any garage or swap meet sale. But there are a few things to be mindful of when offering custom or form fitting products. Keep in mind that a bowling ball might have been cut and sized for a certain type person. If a man is about to make a purchase on a child's bowling ball because he likes its color, and he intends to use it himself, explain to him that it simply wouldn't fit him. Archery bows come in left and right handed versions. Skates (ice and roller), snow skis, bowling shoes, and other size-related items that require custom fit should be plainly marked as such. Golf clubs come in men's and women's styles and left or right handed. Surfboards come in exact lengths and widths; there is always a buoyancy factor to consider with surfboards. They are designed to carry a rider within a specific weight range. Make sure that you do not sell a small board that would sink under the weight of a giant. Make size lists of your custom fit sporting equipment.

Flashlights. Why is it that every time I try to turn on a flashlight, I must beat it against something to get it to work? Even new ones. Invariably your customers will commence to beating on your flashlights, too. It seems to be standard procedure. Even when I know flashlights are working, they still don't work for the public. Well, can't win 'em all!

Mattresses and box springs. I did not say frames and headboards, I said the other. Used mattresses and box springs have a standard life expectancy. They get very dirty, lumpy and foul smelling. Rightfully so, the customers just don't want to buy these products used. They are hygiene-related items and sanitation is important to the consumer when considering these purchases. They are private and intimate considerations for the household.

Prescription items. Medicine is a don't sell item. Prescription medicines that are meant for someone else are just that: meant for someone else. You have to be a licensed pharmacist to sell prescription drugs over a counter. A garage sale or swap meet is no place to sell pharmaceuticals of any sort. This applies to non-prescription remedies like aspirin, cold formulas, and other medicines commonly sold at the supermarkets.

Prescription reading glasses are ground and fit for persons who require them. The lenses themselves are of no use to anyone except the original owner.

Many tinted or sunglasses are prescription ground. They would be of no use to the customer who had good vision.

RETURNS, IMITATIONS, AND FAKES

How will you deal with returned merchandise? Promptly, and with as much courtesy as you can convey. Garage and swap meet sales will give you your first lessons in marketing and salesmanship. Your guidelines should be no different than that of the major retail outlets, for there are standards and policies even in the minor sales markets. One such retail outlet has a motto that is identified with their standard policy: SATISFACTION GUARANTEED OR YOUR MONEY CHEERFULLY REFUNDED. Even though you are not a major corporation, and many policies and codes will not apply to you, you must still strive to show professionalism. You see, the customer is always right and always will be. No matter how unfair it seems, or how much it hurts, you must listen and compromise when confronted with dissatisfaction. I don't mean that you should give in, or surrender without evaluating the situation, because each situation will be different. You'll have to consider many variables when confronted with a displeased customer.

You can play it tough and abide strictly to the "As Is" clause, but sometimes this clause can be carried to extremes. Keep in mind that if you refuse to bend to the customer's wishes in all cases, you will be known for your stern and inflexible attitude. This hurts your repeat business. If enough customers are turned away, it is certain that future income will show signs of decline. Too much decline, and business falls off. And there won't be too much that you can do about it, other than to move your sale location. If your garage sales are held out of your home residence, this will be a difficult chore.

If someone should ask you for their money back on a purchase, the reasonable thing to do is to ask them why they are displeased. If the item in question has a mechanical failure, or the buyer insists that it does, make an honest repair effort. Sometimes a buyer is unfamiliar with the operation of an item. Sometimes the item requires a different hook-up operation in the buyer's home. Perhaps extra parts are needed to adapt the item over to the buyer's system.

A case in point would be a VCR. Suppose you sold a customer a VCR that was originally hooked up in your house. It might have been hooked up using the flat twin lead antenna wire. The buyer might have a coaxial cable supplied with the TV unit, and he could therefore be confused about the proper way to connect it. If the VCR was sold without the converter boxes or adapters, this would also make installation difficult. The buyer would be stuck with his coaxial cable wondering how to adapt it to the VCR. Without instructions or the extra adapters, it is doubtful that he could figure it out himself.

It is at this time that you should assist him, making every effort possible to adapt the VCR over to his system. If you have left out a converter box, or an A/B switch in the sale, you might offer to share the expense of one of these inexpensive adapters with the buyer. Perhaps the buyer has an indoor TV antenna (rabbit ears), and the wires are not long enough to reach the VCR. In this case he would need an antenna block. You could offer to pick one up for him at the local TV shop after you have concluded your sale.

Another ticklish item happens to be typewriters. Electric typewriters are extremely good sales items, but there are so many things that can go wrong with them. Just one inoperable function out of the many is all that is needed for a customer to come back with a complaint. It could be anything from a jammed key to a problem with the proportional spacing. If you can remedy the problem with a few adjustments, do so. If not, it would be advised that you refund the customer's money, put the machine aside, and have it checked out later by an expert.

The point to all of this is that you always show the customer that you are agreeable to following up on your goods. You are not a service center with endless tools and knowledge at your disposal, but rather a concerned seller, who does not want to stick anyone with something that presents problems and further expense.

If a customer insists on a refund, comply. The item in question could be in perfect working order, and the reason for the refund could be a different matter entirely. The buyer might suddenly realize that the money he has spent on a purchase was money that was owed to another source. Only he had forgotten. Caught in an embarrassing situation, and kicking himself for making a foolish buy, he decides to return to you for a refund. Maybe he even seems a little rushed or angry. Whatever the reasons, they are his reasons, and he is due courtesy. This happens with children a lot. They buy at a sale, only to be told by their parents, "Take it back, now!" When this happens, and it will, be agreeable and understand.

Remember the inventory list? It could come in real handy in a return situation. Let's say that a customer returns with an item and demands a prompt refund. He says that he paid such and such for the item a couple of hours ago. Only you think that his refund price doesn't sound right. So you check your inventory list and there it is in black and white; the price he did pay for the item. Only your figure is lower than his. Maybe in the confusion, the customer is mistaken, or maybe not. It is your job to protect your interest by showing him that he is wrong. You have the written proof. His further accusations and denials are from then on groundless. In a small claims court, the evidence would be in your favor. The customer would have to prove malicious intent. Since there is none, only a mix-up about the return price, the case falls in your favor.

"Imitation is the sincerest form of flattery." Or so they say. We try to understand the logic in this phrase, but sometimes it is a little hard to swallow. Product imitations are attempts to approach the original in popularity, appeal, and quality. We know that a product that is extremely popular, produced by a successful manufacturer, is often copied or imitated. There are many reasons for this, but chiefly we can assume that the imitator is desirous of cashing in on some of the huge profits made by the original manufacturer. It can be a popular trend or fad in clothing, or it can be associated with the multi-billion dollar computer industry. Imitation, in its lesser form, is a blatant rip-off, bordering on copyright and trademark infringement. In its highest form, it is an attempt to approach, but not duplicate, a quality in a product that is admired and sought after by the consumer. In any form, imitation does exist nowadays, more so than ever.

If authentic brand names are important to you, then you should know what sets some imitation brands aside from their authentic counterparts. Here is where the product guidebooks come in handy. Especially in the collector categories: antiques, paintings, autographs, sculpture, and other related art products. The collector could stand to lose hundreds, possibly thousands of dollars in these areas, since a great deal of money can be made imitating products that carry large asking prices. The field of jewelry and precious gems is a very dark and forbidding chasm for the amateur to enter. It would nearly take a certified gemologist to differentiate between the myriads of stone cuts alone. This is discounting the different grades that stones and gems come in today. Measurements and weights for determining value are a subject in itself. Most of us cannot tell the true difference between a finely cut zirconium diamond and that of the real McCoy! That is because imitation in the jewelry industry has become an exacting science, so precise that grades and tolerances are designed with such perfection that they baffle even the experts.

Imitators are as far reaching as the food industry. In processed and packaged foods, there are fillers, syrups, colorings, imitation flavors, and aromas that are meant to approach in texture, taste, and smell, the original. These imitations have become so standard that we don't think about it as often as we should.

In general, a good way to tell an original from an imitation is the price. The original will almost always be higher, sometimes by as much as ninety percent, as in the case of exotic perfumes. Another way to tell the difference will be in the labeling. Some imitators will come so close to the original spelling in the product, that at a glance, you will not be able to tell the difference. And many people who are not altogether sure of the original spelling pick up the imitation, thinking that it is the original or that it's close enough. Men have a terrible time in this kind of shopping, especially when confronted with perfumes, colognes, women's clothing, purses and handbags, jewelry, and other designer products.

The laws governing trademark and copyright are sometimes obscure and finely lettered. But as a general rule, it is an infringement to duplicate a manufacturer's product (that has been so protected) in exact form and substance. Sometimes the differences are so subtle that you will not be able to tell with a visual inspection. Then you will have to know the difference by examining the materials and ingredients included in the labeling. If they are not included, then perhaps the only way to tell is in the operating quality of the product. For instance, musical instruments, especially guitars, are copied so closely that their tinny tonal quality is the only thing that gives them away. Thanks to recent laws, in the case of musical instruments the manufacturers have been required to incorporate the word "copy" or "copy cat" into the brand name. For example, Gibson Copy.

In products like purses, handbags, luggage, and shoes the imitators go to great pains to nearly duplicate the outward physical appearance of the product. In doing so, they skimp in areas of quality. You will see poor stitching in the imitations, the absence of lining, and a general overall appearance of poor workmanship. The materials used in imitations are not of the highest quality. The materials look the same, but they will not wear the same. Most imitation tennis shoes fall apart after a year of wear, where the original might last up to three or four years. All too frequently shoe and handbag straps break on the imitated varieties. Glue is used where stitches should be. Sometimes nylon zippers are used where metal ones are called for.

Imitation can be downright fanatical. When it approaches the children's markets, it is a sure sign of desperation. Frequently, toys or stuffed animals that have become legends created by the movie industry have become so popular that the original has gotten lost in the shuffle. In the case of the ET doll, the imitators were not even concerned about making a product that looked like it. Many of the imitations of ET were just vague resemblances — rushed half-attempts. This was, no doubt, to get in on the craze as soon as possible. These manufacturers succeeded in making thousands of dollars on the cheap replicas.

This also applies to the popular movie star dolls that have been cranked out on hurried assembly lines. Certainly, a customer is hard-pressed to know who the original manufacturer of these dolls is. That is, if the original manufacturer is still around producing them. Imitators have a nasty habit of forcing the original parent companies to discontinue production, for reasons of pressure and excessive competition.

IBM has been forced to endure some of the worst competitive pressure of all the corporations combined. Long admired for its high standards and quality workmanship, IBM has come to the realization that they will be cloned and copied from now on, unless drastic measures are taken. IBM has used tremendous efforts in security, and design and development, only to find that it has had little effect. The computer world is just too dependent upon IBM to let them slip off into their own corner and quietly do what they want. IBM has set national standards and developed a huge business following. The imitators have realized this, and would like to have a piece of the action.

It bears repeating that you must always research your specific product needs before a purchase. You are responsible for your own leg work. The following is a small list of some typical products and brand names that have been imitated or copied. Devise your own list. Make it thorough, because you will need it sooner or later.

Computers — IBM, MacIntosh
Handbags and purses — Gucci Luggage
Musical instruments (guitars) — Richenbacher, Fender, Gibson
Perfumes — Giorgio, White Shoulders, Chanel No. 5, Opium
Tennis shoes — Nike, Reebok
Software (computer)
Sunglasses — CoolRay
Toys — Cabbage Patch Kids, Barbie dolls, Lego Building Blocks
Watches — (most popular brand names)

Fakes are more of a trap to the buyer than the seller. The chances of finding a fake or "doctored up" item are very slight, and appropriately, worth only the slightest mention. My definition of a fake is an item that is sold that is minus some or all of its internal workings. This could be a television set with parts of it chassis missing, a small engine minus some vital engine parts, or an electrical appliance with its motor removed. In fact, a fake is a shell or a pretty face with no substance to it. It can be a finely handcarved cuckoo clock, with no mechanism or cuckoo bird inside. It could be a radio with its internal speaker missing. For whatever the reason, internal parts have been removed or sabotaged — the item ends up useless.

Beware of extremely light items that appear to have been gutted. An item that rattles when picked up might be evidence that it was dismantled and hastily put back together. Obviously, an item that doesn't work properly needs further investigation. This is where a request for a demonstration could warn the customer against a bad purchase.

SELLER RESPONSIBILITY

In all cases, the seller has a responsibility to himself and to his customer, if he intends to make a steady profit. To this day, no one has set moral and ethical standards for the modern salesperson, since everyone is different in their approach to making money through sales. In more negative terms they are called tactics — bait and switch, hard sell, pressure. But the fact remains, without some kind of moral guidelines the seller is sure to slip up, and if he goes too far he will be found out for what he truly is: an opportunist bent on greed, with no feelings for others. And in today's market it is getting more difficult to deceive the public. The public is becoming more observant and shrewd in their buying habits. The public is asking more legitimate questions; rightly so, since markets and products are becoming more confusing. Here are some topics and areas that the seller should consider when dealing with the public.

□ When applicable, ask permission to hang up banners, flyers, and signs. Remember to remove them after your sale is over.

□ Don't sell food or soft drinks unless you are a licensed vendor for such products. This also goes for prescription and non-prescription medicines of any sort.

□ Don't sell tobacco, liquor, firearms, fireworks, weapons, or any other age restricted merchandise to minors.

□ Don't sell goods at extremely high prices. Remember that the average department store runs occasional discounts from twenty-five to forty percent off list price on new items. Are you running at about forty percent off, or better?

□ Don't knowingly sell stolen or borrowed merchandise. It can only hurt you in the long run. If you do, you're liable to be reported for such business and prosecuted.

□ Don't sell fake or doctored up merchandise. It is useless to the consumer and a detriment to your character.

□ Don't sell handguns at garage sales or general goods swap meets. Reserve these items for specialty advertising in the shopping magazines. The exception would be a gun show.

□ Keep sale items on your property or within your booth area.

□ Be careful when selling pets. Exclude exotic or wild animals from your sale.

☐ Is most of your merchandise in working order? Have you made every effort to locate instructions and directions for items that require them?

☐ Be mindful when selling motor vehicles. Is all of the paperwork in order according to the Department of Motor Vehicles?

☐ Have you given full credit to the people who have consigned goods to you? Make sure that you return all unsold consignment goods. Pay off all consignments promptly.

☐ Don't make promises to a customer that you can't keep. Don't tell a customer that you will make it up to him next week just because he missed out on that deal today. Don't guarantee the delivery of that item if you cannot deliver.

☐ Do you have enough change on hand? Have plenty of pocket change, ones, fives, tens, and a few twenty dollar bills.

☐ Are you ready to fully demonstrate mechanical hardware? Do you have extension cords and electrical outlets readily available? You will need them to run electrically operated merchandise.

☐ Remember to be patient and show equal consideration to all people, especially children.

☐ Are you being mindful of your neighbors or fellow booth vendors by keeping your radio down? Remember that heavy drinking and abusive language is a turn off to the public and those around you.

☐ Always remember that goods belonging to the Salvation Army and Goodwill Industries are the rightful property of these foundations. Just because it's gathered around their collection sites is no reason to assume that it is free for the taking.

SMALL BUSINESS AND TAXES

First, I must explain that I am not a tax expert, nor do I profess to have most of the answers that you will need when considering the topics of this book as a small business venture. Every small business requires specialized attention. There are so many variables involved. Each state has its own way of preparing taxes — different forms for different applications. So basically, we will discuss the general federal income tax stipulations along with a few other areas of importance and how they will apply to your situation. My advice, at the forefront, is to consult a tax expert for the specialized information that you will need.

In the first place, in considering part-time garage sales as a recognized and legitimate business, the answer will have to be no. It is doubtful that anybody makes their entire and/or exclusive income from everyday garage sales, much less part-time involvement. And that is what garage sales are slated to be: somewhere along the lines of the word "hobby," or supplemental income. The IRS requires a legitimate business to be one in which you can show a profit in a three out of five year period. The fact that you are using your driveway as an area for business is also against you, since their definition of business space is a little bit different — something more professionally recognized.

To claim a deduction on a garage sale would mean that your driveway would have to be used exclusively for the purpose of the sale and for no other reason; like parking the car. Most business space that is deductible is defined as office space, work space, or storefront property of some type. Not the pavement area of a driveway as in the case of a private home. Your driveway is not partitioned off with walls, with at least one exit or door, and certainly, you don't spend a great deal of time on your driveway conducting real business.

Expenses incurred while conducting a hobby or "other income" are not deductible, but the money that you make on the sideline is fully taxable. You have to list these extra earnings on a Form 1040. Earnings of over five hundred dollars are generally the amount at which you would begin to report this income and fill out the necessary forms.

Really, the only time that you could claim deductions for a garage sale is if you were entirely self employed in this work, and were equipped with the legitimate business structure as defined by the IRS. Then you would list your business earnings on the appropriate Schedule C. This allows you to deduct any and all reasonable expenses directly associated with the operation of your business. The fact that you would be solely involved in garage sales as a means of support and livelihood is very unlikely. Trying to convince the IRS of this would be a task in itself. As of this date, the new tax laws have further stiffened the qualifications for the small business person. The government's aim is to crack down on and eliminate the cheaters.

However, there is a favorable glitch in all of this. If you use a portion of your home, say an empty bedroom, as a small factory used exclusively for the production of handmade stuffed alligators, and you sell them on your driveway as your only means of income, you would then have a legitimate deduction. The bedroom would be the legitimate business area because the bedroom is now your principal place of work.

Once you have established that you have a legitimate deduction, you will want to know how much it will be. This is figured by square footage; the percentage of the area that the bedroom occupies in regard to the total area of your house. If your home has a total square footage of 3,200 feet, and your bedroom (your factory, now) is 400 square feet, then you could deduct twelve and a half percent from your total rent amount. This is, of course, if you are renting. Your utility bills are also deducted in this manner (twelve and a half percent of the total utility bill), and is reported on Schedule C. Your deductions cannot exceed your gross income.

If you own a home it is a little different. Your deductions for your work space can't be more than your gross income minus the deductions you could have taken anyway if the area wasn't used for business; like real estate taxes and mortgage interest. Also, any repairs that are directly involved with the work space can be deducted like: lighting installation, plumbing, heating, or other necessary repairs. If you have this kind of business setup (and it is rare) you will want to know what else you are entitled to.

Materials incurred for making your product are legitimate deductions. In the case of the alligators, for example, the fabric used for making it, thread, needles, decorations, and even repairs to your sewing machine are all write-offs. If you use stationery or forms for keeping track of accounts, this would be included. Virtually everything directly associated with the business is considered a reasonable deduction.

Any insurance that you have bought to safeguard your business can be deducted. Homeowner's insurance is a qualified deduction.

If you borrow money for business purposes, like making payments on a production machine, your loan interest can be deducted.

All of your postage for business correspondence, answering letters, and mailing your products is deductible.

Other deductions include travel and entertainment, business telephone, operating taxes, business repairs, business publications, and other related expenses.

Once you have all of your business deductions itemized, you total them up and subtract them from your business income. This will give you the net profit from your business during the year. This information goes on the 1040 and Schedule SE.

Self-employment tax will be a double whammy, for you. As a self-employed business person you will have to pay an employers share and your own share of your Social Security Tax. You will use the SE to figure your self-employment tax. Enter the net profit from Schedule C on the appropriate line indicated. At least there is a maximum that the government can charge for Social Security tax; the figure varies and you will have to look it up.

Naturally, since you are self-employed the government does not withhold regular earnings from you. So the government has what is called an estimated tax. This requires you to guess at how much income you will receive in a given year. You must pay taxes on it in advance in quarterly payments. Failure to pay the tax when it is due results in a penalty plus interest on the overdue time that was taken to pay it.

The Keogh Plan is helpful for the small business person who has another regular job. You can put aside fifteen percent of your self-employment income or $7500, whichever is less, in a Keogh plan. Whatever you put aside is then deducted from your total net income on the 1040; this lowers your gross income. The lower your income, the less tax you will have to pay. This way, at least you will be earning interest. Beware though, there are strict penalties for subtracting money from this special account. It is not to be tampered with. The interest that you earn in this type of account is tax free at the time that you earn it. Different banks have different varieties of this account available. Some yield high interest and some yield low interest. It is advised that you contact the proper authority to tailor an account for you that meets your specific needs.

The professional swap meet vendor has it a little easier when it comes to legitimate deductions. Many swap meet vendors have state resale licenses and conduct their sales on a regular basis. Many of them do make their sole living from area and booth sales. It is easier for them to prove that they have a bona fide work space at home that is designated for the storage or assembly of wholesale items. Many times the space turns out to be an office that is used for the accounting in the business. Most often the professional vendors will have a city business license as well as a state wholesale license number. When these vendors sell to other businesses, those businesses report their purchases at tax time which forces the vendor to pay taxes on profits whether he likes it or not.

Indoor swap meets, which commonly carry insurance, are favorite sale sites for the professional vendors. Booth and area space can cost from $100.00 to $250.00 and up at these mass market extravaganzas. It is usually a requirement, at the indoor varieties, to sell new or remanufactured goods, thus requiring a wholesale license. This booth or area rental is fully deductible as an expense incurred while conducting professional business. Travel expense going to and from is allowable as a deduction. The same with advertisements, business cards, and other related expenditures.

Again, the tax experts are fully qualified to advise you on all of your possible deductions. Follow their advice and do pay taxes. It is no secret that many small business persons understate their yearly income reports. Some of these same people even duck taxes altogether. The chances of getting caught are slim, but the risks are too great to chance it. If you fall under an audit, there is a chance that your future activities will be monitored. It is an uneasy feeling when you suspect that big brother might be watching. The way to keep the big eye from falling on you is to pay the taxes and be done with it.

Chapter Eleven

ANTIQUES AND COLLECTIBLES

My, What Old Things You Have

The greatest hidden treasures to be found at garage sales and swap meets are antiques and collectibles. Authentic antiques and collectibles are sound investments, in addition to being purchases that reward and gratify. There are serious collectors of every type and position in society in every nation of the globe. Some are general collectors. Others specialize in one or more of the many collecting fields: clocks, crystal, baseball cards, tobacco tins, bottles, rugs, paintings, sculptures, coins, stamps, pottery, lamps, weapons, and old documents. The popularity of antiques and collectibles has not declined at all, but has shown a marked increase in sales and devotees. Antiques and collectibles are not only a fascinating hobby, they are an excellent opportunity to make substantial profits on mediocre investments. Out of all the areas of bargain hunting they are probably the most interesting and challenging endeavor.

Antiques and collectibles cover a wide array of objects and time periods. It will be your decision to study and learn a little bit about everything, or a lot about a few areas. In either case, you will want to obtain the latest literature and guidebooks in your chosen field. For example, if you have collected some dolls and you would like to try your hand at some restoration, you would find copies of *Bambini* magazine and *The Dollmaker* magazine very useful. Don't fear that you will miss out on all the great deals if you happen to specialize. As with anything worth knowing, you will develop a keen eye and the special skill needed to spot most great bargains in the field of antiques and collectibles.

There is always a new generation of collectors cropping up who have a lot of cash and a short time to spend it. If you are known as an occasional seller of antiques and collectibles, you will find that an exclusive group of people will

Porcelain collectibles

be willing to seek you out on a regular basis. People drive far and wide for choice antiques. Collecting is a serious business to them. Their fandom borders on the fanatical. They desire to be the first on the scene in order to vacuum up as many old and dear relics as possible. Sell just one Chippendale chair and the word will be out — you carry antiques. Sell two or three — you're a source, an authority! There is an advantage to selling antiques and collectibles in a sale, even if you sell only one or two. People who shop antiques and collectibles are intensely loyal. They are liable to have more money than the average shopper. They will make it a point to contact you at regular intervals to ask if you have something special in your inventory. As shoppers, they are fiercely competitive with each other, and many of their purchases are made on the spur of the moment. Intellectually you will find them the most engaging and fascinating of any group. Who else could hold your undivided attention for two hours explaining the history of bottle caps?

We will lump the buyer and seller together in this chapter since the strategies for obtaining antiques and collectibles will be the same. The seller will have to be a buyer first before he can begin to appreciate the effort it takes to find choice pieces. Many antique and collectible buyers are traders and sellers, so really, the two are one and the same.

THE HUNT

The first thing that you must consider is what objects and periods fascinate you. If you limit yourself to two or three areas you are likely to learn more specific details. Your selection might be based on the fact that you already have a few pieces of let's say, Derby porcelain. So this might start out at the top of your list. Perhaps your neighbor has a large antique bottle collection, and you might be able to make a deal for some of them. Maybe you have always had a fascination with stamps, but you know little or nothing about them. So there you have it — three areas that would be a good starting frame for you. What's your next step? Go to the library and check out a book for each. Not five books for each — one for each subject is sufficient. You don't have to become an expert on the subjects, but you do want to acquire a basic understanding of what you are getting into in terms of cost, availability, and resale value. You will want to know what kind of present day prices you can fetch for your pieces. You will want to know what kind of prices your pieces can expect to demand on tomorrow's market. The following lists are three areas of antiques and collectibles:

RECOGNIZED GENERAL ANTIQUES

English furniture up to 1840
Silver, glass, crystal, china, sculptures
Pre-1900 signed original oil paintings

American Colonial, Shaker, and
Federal Victorian Furniture

COLLECTIBLES

Cameras	Tools
Watches	Farming equipment
Indian artifacts	Bottles
Toys	Glassware
Quilts and rugs	Cans (produce)
Lamps	Telescopes
Stoves	Appliances
Art deco 1920-30	Plates
Mission Oak	Stamps
Jewelry	Coins and currency
Dolls	Games and puzzles
Miniatures	Newspapers and magazines
Weaponry	Books
Fire extinguishers	Trains (hobby toys)
Clocks	

PRESENT DAY COLLECTIBLES (Collectibles of tomorrow)

Baseball/football cards	Beer cans
Soft drink bottles/cans	Tokens
Dolls (movie star)	Comic books
Small press books	Small press magazines
Movie posters	Autographs
Marbles	Pins and buttoms (presidential)

Present Day Collectibles (continued)

Record albums	Bicycles and wagons
Ship models	Newspapers
Radios	Figurines (limited edition)
Plates (commemorative)	

Be sure that you obtain the latest pricing guidebooks for your particular antique or collectible. A publication that is over three years old is nearly out of date since prices are subject to rapid change and interest. What was hot six months ago could be old hat at the present. Prices listed in the guidebooks are often estimates. This is because the condition of a piece plays a crucial part in its actual worth. It is unfortunate, but to this day, antiques and collectibles are based on a "guestimate" type of pricing, unlike coins, which have very precise and defined terms for condition, age, and wear. Talking with other people who share the same specialty area as you can aid you in determining your own asking prices.

You can start your hunt by visiting antique shops and auctions. You won't dig right in and start buying things. Your first excursions should be confined to getting used to the surroundings and talking to as many authorities as you can. This is to gain some insight in how the buying and trading of antiques and collectibles is done. Take a notebook with you so you can record vital information like: which items are popular and command the highest prices; which items hold their value more; what publications are the best source guides; what flea markets or swap meets sell antiques and collectibles exclusively. Hobnob with the dealers and auctioneers.

An excellent source for finding your treasures will be in your own family circle of friends and relatives. If relatives or family members find that they have pieces that have no sentimental value or need to be disposed of, they are more likely to surrender them to a family member. Grandmothers and grandfathers are a great source for antiques and collectibles. Grandparents are the relatives most likely to have saved family heirlooms and mementos. That doesn't mean that you should rush up to them with that "Okay, give!" attitude. A little persuasion would work best, in this case. Telling your grandparents honestly what your intentions are is the best way to gain their favor and trust.

Establish a good rapport with local dealers and shop owners. There is a good chance that you will be dealing with them more than once, so make a good first impression. Most dealers and shop owners do not object to honest questions coming from a curious mind. It is best to be up front with them and tell them that you are just starting out. They will delight in tutoring you since they were once beginners, and you represent a potential customer. Listen attentively to what they have to tell you. Do some brain picking — take notes if you must.

THE KILL

Once you have gained a little experience in the field you will want to go out and make your first kill: a kill being a steal, or great buy. Looking for a purchase the first time out, it might be best to scout the flea markets and garage sales. It would be difficult to make a killing at an antique shop. A good buy, yes. A killing, no. This is because most dealers and shop owners are well aware of their inventory and the prices that they expect to get. It is unlikely that you could talk a dealer down from an established and set price.

To make a killing you're going to have to have prey. So what in the heck are you going to look for? If it smells old do you buy it? Purchases have been made for less, especially where antiques and collectibles are concerned. So much of this type of buying is done with "gut instinct" that there are really no hard and fast rules — if there were, we would all be experts! But to make things easy on yourself, do a little research first on furniture. There is still a lot of antique furniture out there. Study the illustrated antique guidebooks and pay particular attention to the photos and artwork of the furniture pieces. Stare, stare, stare, at the pictures, then read the captions. If you are artistically inclined, sketch the furniture to give you some feel for the different shapes and contours.

When en route to garage sales or flea markets, and if you have a color guidebook, bring it with you. If the sale has numerous pieces of antique furniture stand to the side and open your book. Then flip pages and identify, flip pages and identify, flip and identify! If you recognize a piece that you have found in your book, repeat the name of the piece out loud to yourself, over and over again, if you have to. This will force your mind to identify and trigger a response mechanism if you see the piece again. You might lose a sale standing there blabbering to yourself, but you can walk away with the conviction that, "Hey, I know and recognize three pieces of furniture, real good!" At your next sale you might not have to refer to your book to recognize a piece, but instead be able to call it up from memory. Then you could buy if you wish, safe in the knowledge that you have a little background on it. This method works like the flash card principle. I've used it many times, being an amateur enthusiast myself.

Let's take a look at some furniture pieces and periods. There will be some characteristics that are exclusive to each.

The Gothic style came into being from about 1200 to 1600. Later, it appeared again: eighteenth century (Chippendale Gothic); early nineteenth (Regency Gothic); late nineteenth century (Victorian). Arches, columns, foliage, the human figure, and a general embroidered look, can be found on furniture of this period. The plain examples of this furniture might have decorative straps, plates, and hinges of mostly iron. The earlier period chests and coffers will be of plank construction, that is, boards or slats joined with nails or pins.

The chairs made during this period were regal looking with high backs and box seats. The arms were enclosed giving them a wrapped-in look.

Louis XVI armchair, French

The tables were often massive and designed to accommodate many diners. They usually came in sections, so they could be dismantled within a castle. The table top sat on huge trestle-like legs.

The Victorian Gothic pieces of the later nineteenth century are more likely to be found in great numbers at garage sales and flea markets. There were many more of these pieces produced. The earlier Gothic period furniture has become widely spread, and although not impossible to find at garage sales and flea markets, the pieces are more often in the hands of dealers, and seen at the auctions.

The Renaissance style began about 1400, its roots in Italy. The pieces were massively constructed, often inlaid with colored stones and sometimes gems.

Renaissance-style carved walnut cabinet 1860

The chest was a popular item, generally box-like in shape, with curving fronts and ends. They were made chiefly of walnut and cypress. They were ornately carved and sometimes painted with religious scenes on the top, front, and sides.

The French versions of Renaissance furniture emerged with the Dressoir: a cupboard atop a stand or platform; and the two-part cupboard carved with half-human figures that served as foundations. These cupboards are very popular today and command the highest asking prices.

French writing desk

The Elizabethan four-poster bed is a choice piece to find, as are the Farthingdale chairs, which were rather square looking and without armrests. Before 1600 such chairs were not made in sets but in singles.

Early American coffer-type chests showed a lack of detail as opposed to their foreign counterparts, but were popular nonetheless. Nicholas Disbrowe from England built many of them while in residence in Connecticut. He signed the front of them with a tulip design. Other chest craftsmen of note were John Allis from Hadley and Samuel Belding of Hatfield, Connecticut. These chests were made from oak, chiefly, with elm and ash reserved for the final finishing woods.

Two traditional chairs of note during this period were the Carver, with a row of spindles in the back; and the Brewster, which had a double row. Some were made of all wood, and some had fabric and rush seats. The availability of these chairs today is good, and the beginning collector would fare well in obtaining one.

American spindle back

The Baroque style which began in Italy, used a wide variety of materials to achieve exaggerated effects. Baroque merely means strange beauty. Some of the forms included the S-shape, twisting curves, or looped decorations. Veneering became popular; the process of overlaying a base wood with a thin sheet of finely textured wood, as did marquetry and parquetry. Marquetry is a design that is inset using many veneers into a base work of veneer. Parquetry is known for its geometric designs, squares, rectangles, triangles, and other formations of wood pieces that look three-dimensional.

Spanish baroque desk with leather tooled chairs

Baroque style chairs were tall with arching backs, while their seats were narrower. Often, the chair legs were ornately carved and ended in a claw or paw.

From the late seventeenth century the English and American pieces of furniture were constructed in a double deck fashion; one piece sitting atop the other. Among these, the highboy and secretary desk are two examples.

Throughout the eighteenth century drawer handles were often made of brass, giving the furniture an air of distinction. Original brass work has always been considered an added feature when found intact and in good condition on the finer pieces.

Queen Anne dining set

In the Rococo style during the Queen Anne period, English and American furniture grew more subdued. The styles mellowed with a more graceful or feminine accent on sculptured motif. Shells, flowers, foliage, vines, ribbons and bows, and other intricate designs were used in place of the more traditional straight lines. Surfaces were veneered in exotic woods, and many of these pieces were beyond the means of the average person. The French craftsmen also made a superb inventory of tables and desks, chairs and settees, and drawer-type chests during this period.

Chinese Chippendale is characterized by chairs with square backs and lattice-type arms. Carved and gilt mirrors were popular with figures of mandarins, dragons, pagodas, garden scenes, and birds.

Rose inlaid mother of pearl corner chair (Oriental)

The Neoclassic style was a return to the more conventional straight lines, ovals, circles, and square backs. Still, the excavations of Pompeii and Herculaneum sparked an interest in the classical column, the urn, the animal head, the trophy of arms, and the semi-nude human figure.

Most of the old standard pieces endured: the flat top writing table, the lady's desk, the arm chair, and the arm chair with padded back rest. The modest works with more plain designs were Pembroke tables, toilet mirrors, chairs with square tapered legs, and combination cupboard and drawer gentlemen's wardrobes. Mahogany furniture with simpler lines existed for those with more modest budgets.

Oak hall tree (American)

George Hepplewhite is generally known for his unique interpretation of a style known as French Hepplewhite. The chair backs were mostly oval, shield, or heart-shaped. On quality Hepplewhite furniture carvings of pendant husks, bell flowers, and feathers are in evidence. He might well have been the original designer of the sideboard as a single unit of furniture: the drawer cupboard combination. The American style of Federal furniture had heavy influence from John Seymour of Boston, Samuel McIntire of Salem, and Matthew Egerton of New Jersey.

The Empire style was characterized by its glorification of Rome, Egypt, and Greece. This brought about chairs with saber legs, couches with upturned feet and scrolled end work. A vast amount of this type of furniture was produced by French craftsmen from Paris.

In England the styles were known as English Empire or Regency, which lasted from 1800 to 1830. These pieces were less ornate than the French versions but still revealed some remarkable workmanship. Some of the pieces included sofa tables with end flaps, chairs with turned legs, round tables with single, pyramid-shaped column supports, and small bookcases with grill-worked doors. A lot of brass was used to decorate and form stark contrasts. Duncan Phyfe, a Scottish-born American, excelled in this style with the X-shaped base for chairs and tables. His interpretation of the Grecian style sofa was very popular at the time.

Duncan Phyfe desk/buffet

*American Chippendale
(claw foot)*

Victorian pump organ

The Victorian style encompassed all of the other periods with its own unique look. Some of the nineteenth century fashions were quite extravagant in appearance but many of the pieces had an elegant quality, especially the drawing room furniture. John Belter of New York City made many center tables and console tables with marble tops.

Attention to extravagant ornamentation was not the intention of a religious group called the Shakers. Their furniture appeared in America and England during the nineteenth century. It was distinguished by its simplicity and regular features. The Shakers' attention to detail was confined mostly to careful workmanship, precise fit, and practicality. Their furniture was always plain-looking, minus brass handles and fixtures or any other type of sophisticated decorations.

Pine cabinet atop chest of drawers — indicative of Shaker design

CONSIDERATIONS AND VALUES

Once you find what you consider a good buy you will need a strategy when approaching the seller. It can be summed up very simply. The whole idea will be to buy low and sell high. Since this will be the intention of the seller as well, you will find yourself at the haggling crossroad again. Have a precise idea of what the maximum or top market value is on a piece before you buy it. *The Antique Trader Weekly* and the *Maine Antique Digest* are two major publications that can help you in determining current value. You wouldn't want to pay $500.00 for a New Haven schoolhouse clock if you knew that its true collecting value according to present day information was $200.00.

Just as important is the need to check and see if all of the original parts of an antique are present and have not been replaced with remanufactured substitutes. Examine the furniture wood carefully. The coloration and wood material should be uniform throughout. A mahogany dropleaf table with one of the leaves made of pine would be a sure indication that an original part was replaced with substandard material. This modification would subtract heavily from the table and its true antique value.

Many antique pieces of furniture have lost their original frame strength due to age and weathering, or being constantly moved about. In most cases minor repairs are within the capability of the amateur. A few nails, pins, and a container of good woodworking glue is all that is needed to set some pieces right. For instance, a spindle back chair with a few loose spindles can be easily repaired with a little clear-drying wood glue. Heavy restoration and refinishing should be avoided if at all possible. This is because evidence of such reworking is easily spotted by a professional, and it does lower original antique value. Major reconstruction, i.e., changing parts and adding new fittings, is likened to tampering and many serious collectors frown on this. The idea is to purchase an authentic piece that is as near to original condition as possible. The only time that major restoration would be justified is in the case of extremely rare one-of-a-kind pieces.

Minor restoration or "prep" is certainly warranted but this is no more involved than cleaning with mineral spirits, followed by a heavy application of paste wax to protect both the original finish and the wood underneath. Completely stripping the entire piece of its original finish should only be considered as a last resort. Or if the original finish is so worn that the wood is in jeopardy of suffering the elements, then complete refinishing would not only enhance the piece, but save it from deterioration. Furniture probably allows the most leeway when restoration is needed. Where it gets a bit tricky is with such items as clocks, watches, music boxes, and musical instruments.

A two hundred and fifty year old bracket clock that has a broken movement will not fetch full value. The cost of such a clock, broken or not, might be prohibitive to the average collector, but the repair of such a piece, provided an expert could be found to do the work, would be bone chilling. The restoration repair might cost two or three times the amount that was paid for the clock. Sure, you say that you picked up an American square piano circa 1850 for three hundred dollars, but did you remember that it was sold at that price because several of its strikers were crushed and broken? Where are you going to find an expert restorer who can do such repair work? And hold onto your hat, how much is it going to cost you if you do find the proper repair expert? What is the parts availability for such a piece? Will broken pieces have to be custom or handmade? Are you aware of the expense involved in custom antique restoration? Can you afford it? Think the matter over carefully before you go out and buy an antique with mechanical workings. You will find that most of the original companies do not exist anymore. If you find one that does exist, what assures you that they will have your needed part in stock?

AUCTIONS

Auctions are where the true market value of antiques and collectibles is tested. Auctions are fast paced, confusing at times, and very unpredictable, especially for the newcomer. There is a heavy gambling air associated with auctions. It is the only place where a wide cross-section of buyers actually determines the final market value (selling price) of whatever is bid on. If you want to buy at an auction, all you have to do is be the one with the last and highest bid. It is very possible to get better than retail prices at auctions, but your timing will have to be superb and you must possess nerves of steel. A lot of ready money helps too.

The common farm auction is still alive and well in the rural areas of the nation. Though farm auctions are primarily known for the sale of tools, machinery, and farming implements, it is not impossible to find some quality pieces of old furniture in the diggings. There is an atmosphere of desperation associated with farm auctions and the prices are apt to be better with the more general items. An old butter churn might be considered secondary by the owner, thus kicked aside and forgotten until some buyer with a keen eye happens along and makes an offer on it. It is these little unexpected finds that are the true treasures of any auction.

The indoor antique auctions attract very large crowds since they are often advertised widely by the sponsors. The public can sit because chairs are often provided and they can watch a multitude of items pass before their eyes, making bids if they want to, or just acting out the part of the observer. The serious dealers and shop owners attend the indoor events, since they realize that the inventory will be larger, thus the selection better.

The private auction or estate sale is becoming more and more popular. Instances in which the entire inventory of a home or estate is sold in a very short time are common. If the home or estate happens to belong to nobility or a celebrity, the chances of finding exquisite pieces are all that much better. Sometimes professional auctioneers are brought in to run these events, sometimes it is the owner who runs the festivities and calls for bids. You might even find complimentary wine served, but keep a clear head — things always look rosier when you've lifted a glass in toast.

Regardless of the type of auction you attend, you will always want to make a pre-sale inspection if one is provided. In the case of private or estate auctions, arriving early to check out the inventory will help you to determine what is worth bidding on and what is not. This early arrival can also assist you with some last minute research before the actual bidding starts. With the larger indoor auctions you can expect to find the date and time of pre-sale inspection in their initial advertisement. And upon arriving at the pre-sale you may find many of the pieces being unloaded, uncrated, and prepared for sale.

Take notes at the pre-sale. Remember which pieces are in mint condition, and take note of the ones with obvious flaws. This is your time to inspect things close up and carefully, because you will not get this chance on the actual auction day. Determine then and there what your top bid offer will be—record it, and make sure that you stick to it when the time comes.

As confusing as they seem, auctions still proceed in an orderly fashion. You will be assigned a number by a staff member and be required to register, supplying them with identification. Once the auction gets under way the auctioneer will, by use of a chant, begin taking bids on merchandise that is usually passed from one end of a stage to the other. The merchandise will be auctioned from tables or lots, and these will also be assigned numbers. To participate in the bidding you have merely to wave your hand or hold up your bid card so that assistants can see it and acknowledge you. To make a purchase on an item you must be the last bidder with the highest offer, and it will be at this time that a clerk will record your number and turn the information over to the cashier. At the end of the auction you visit the cashier, pay for your purchases, and take them home. Just remember to take your bid card with you or destroy it on the spot. If you throw it down or leave it before the auction is over, someone could pick it up and use it, crediting you with purchases that you have not made.

The reason an auctioneer speaks the way he does, often sounding like a rapid fire alien, is because he wants to keep your attention. People rarely fall asleep at auctions — they're too busy trying to hear what the auctioneer is saying. Indeed, you have to listen carefully because the bids will proceed in hikes or jumps. It could be five dollar jumps, ten dollar jumps, or more. The auctioneer has every right to refuse a bid that falls between his jump. If a bid is holding at twenty-five dollars, and the jumps have been in fives, your offer of twenty-seven dollars and fifty cents could be declined. Bidding between jumps slows things down. The auctioneer has the right to set the pace, thus his refusal is justified.

There are a few terms that the beginner will want to learn and remember as the auction proceeds:

Choice — This means that the winning bid takes either one or several pieces that are offered up for sale. This is where your pre-sale knowledge comes in handy. If you remembered which, i.e., chair or table, was the pick of the lot, you could certainly use your choice option to buy it and turn down the others.

So much apiece, take all — Many times antiques and collectibles are sold in sets, like dishes, chairs, vases, and lamps. You will be bidding on only one of the examples, but your final paying price will be determined by the total number of pieces in the matching set or group. A dish that you bid on and win for ten dollars might be part of a set of twelve so you must pay the sum of one hundred and twenty dollars for the set.

Large jump bids — Buyers will use this technique against one another. It happens when someone wants to discourage other bidders from participating by offering a very large bid offer, say one hundred dollars or two hundred dollars over the present amount. This kind of bidding is effective in discouraging the not-so-wealthy, since it can push the price of an item up to its near maximum worth. It is not as reckless as it might seem, especially if the one making the large jump bid knows exactly what they can get for the item, above their investment.

Call-ups — This is a practice in which a bidder can call up or request that a certain piece be put up for auction before the regular schedule proceeds any further. This is really only a timesaver for people who don't want to spend the entire day waiting for their favorite pick to be put on the block. Instead, they want a chance to get it over and done with because they are a nervous wreck and can't stand the suspense, or they simply have some other place to go and cannot spend a great deal of time at the auction. This works well if at any time the auction begins to thin. The less competition, the better, especially for a choice piece.

Consignments — Consignments have the same effect in auctions as they do in garage or swap meet sales: they puff up the appearance of a sale by adding extra inventory. Owners of consignment items delight in seeing their merchandise come up for bid. They sometimes jump right into the auction making bids on their own goods, "running the bid up." It's truly their fault when they win out and buy their own item back!

Minimum or set — Many people who consign to auctions request that their goods have a set or minimum price. This is to assure the consignor that he will at least get a certain price for his item if the bids happen to suddenly fall off. Auctioneers sometimes do this by starting a piece off high which is usually the bare minimum price that they feel that they should get.

Buyers ring— This happens when a large group of dealers agrees beforehand to slacken off bids on each other's preferred pieces. It's kind of a "you scratch my back, I'll scratch yours" type pact. Or a "when the time comes on my piece, shut up and let me have it, and I'll do likewise" agreement. This practice is almost like organized crime in the auction business, somewhat like "cornering the market."

Though I have not been to a great many auctions the rumor still persists that at some auctions there can be found plants or shills who are in league with the auctioneer and are part of the audience. It is the plant's responsibility to continue bidding when items threaten to go for less than expected. It is a form of running up the bid, only the auction house is the cause of it. Again, I don't suppose I would know a plant if he looked right at me since I've found myself too busy at auctions. Still, I cannot discount the fact that chicanery could exist at an auction.

The advantage that you will have at the larger auctions is that dealers or shop owners seldom "gang up" and "hog" all of the merchandise. They are very selective as a rule, and careful in their purchases since they are concerned with overhead and good profit margin. They have a certain percentage to make and must abide by rules of purchase that are a little more strict than yours. It is often the beginner who shows his real hind end when he obviously overbids on a piece and finds himself stuck with it. That is why it is a good idea to watch the techniques of the professionals around you. Watch if they make large jumps or follow the natural rhythm of the sale. Watch which items they fight it out for, which ones they win. You might venture to ask a buyer questions when the sale is over. Did he have any regrets? Was there a piece that he truly felt that he missed out on? Why? Perhaps you could ask him, if he was noticing, what you could have done better to further your chances of a successful buy.

Very sensitive people are apt to get flustered or even intimidated at auctions. It takes a cold heart and nerves of steel to look the auctioneer in the face and nod, "Yes" or shake for "No." And if you are into the heat of the bid, battling it out with another buyer, the auctioneer will be focused directly on you, and so will a lot of the audience. This is when you must keep your cool, with all thoughts of the eyes and minds that are seemingly burning into you out of your battle plan. Remember your mission: you have your pre-sale research under your belt along with your fixed price in mind, and nothing should deter you from standing toe to toe with the best of them and trying for all you are worth for that special piece.

Let's hope that you have brought a vehicle to the auction that is suitable to transport the items you have purchased. Most often a truck or a van is sufficient in transporting the light to medium-sized furniture. There could be a real problem when you have been caught up in the sale and become the proud owner of a Steinway baby grand, only to remember that you arrived at the auction in a Honda Civic. Then you would have to make some frantic arrangements to get your piece home. This is where a tape measure, used at the pre-sale, would have helped you in knowing if your vehicle was large enough to accommodate the piece.

Remember to bring some wrapping pads or blankets with you if you do expect to buy and transport furniture. Old pillows serve as good cushions between furniture pieces. Also included in your moving kit would be masking tape, bungy cord or tie-down rope, and perhaps a small red flag to attach to pieces that extend past the rear bumper of your vehicle. Cardboard boxes and newspapers are handy to pack fragile items: porcelain, lamps, dishes, clocks, and sculptures. Exercise care when picking up or lifting antique furniture. It is not as durable as the modern variety, and frequently sags under its own weight. Avoid picking up tables by the leaves, especially if they are extended. Pick up chairs by the seat instead of the back rest. Carry lamps by their bases and not by their shade hoops.

In this chapter you have had but a brief glimmer of one of the most fascinating hobbies or professions you are likely to meet. Listing individual pieces and presenting color plates and artwork are best left to the professionals and their expert publications. Visit your local library and examine the many books and guides that are available. You will not come away disappointed. I wish you the best of luck in your quest and search for hidden treasures.

Chapter Twelve

THE CRAZE OF THE INDOOR SWAP MEET

My, What a Nice House You Have!

Swap meets are not new. For more than three decades they have been part of the nation's retail lifestyle. On the east coast they are commonly called flea markets, but we all know them to be large events where the word "bargain" is the order of the day. They are meant to attract thousands of shoppers, and they do, effortlessly. Some of the grandest events are of the county variety and typically take up dozens of acres, with hundreds of booths, display areas, refreshment stands, and eager sellers, all wanting to snag the contents of your wallet or purse. And they succeed, oh, do they ever succeed! How in the world could anybody top such an event as a county-held swap meet? Well, move over buster because the indoor swap meet has arrived! The colossus is here. The Cadillac of the swap meets threatens to eclipse in magnitude and sheer numbers its baby brothers, who can only stand by and watch in awe as this new concept takes hold and digs its talons deeper into the retail consciousness of the nation.

What were once open fields housing vendors who offered garage sale leftovers, seconds, and used merchandise by the truckload, have evolved into one of the latest retail extravaganzas — the indoor swap meet. Really the name is misleading since used merchandise is associated with the term swap meet. This concept of selling is different with the indoor varieties because new merchandise, and only new merchandise, is sold at indoor swap meets.

Among the most popular indoor swap meets in the nation are in California. Two of them, known as the Valley Indoor Swap Meets, are located in Woodland Hills and Panorama City. Annually drawing more than a million visitors, the Valley Indoor Swap Meets offer higher quality merchandise and a greater variety of goods than is traditionally found in the outdoor meets. This has been a boon to shoppers who have always shied away from meets

Inside the indoor swap meet

Exterior entrance

that offered only used goods. Glenn Malkin, president of Metropolitan Marketing, Inc., has been quoted as saying, "We've created a shopper's paradise, a mecca for the serious bargain hunter."

As the name implies, these meets are held indoors, protected from the sun, wind, and rain. In the case of the Woodland Hills location, it is a converted industrial complex. The Panorama City location is located in the former Ohrbach's department store. The name swap meet was retained in the examples of these two meets because the term is synonymous with bargain prices, and they wanted to attract the already loyal crowd of the regular outdoor meets. But that is where the comparison stops. The owners of such meets stipulate in the vendor's contract that no used merchandise will be sold under any circumstances for any reason. Between the two locations they have over nine hundred individually owned and operated booth displays. The majority of the merchandise carries a regular and familiar brand name.

These types of meets offer designer clothing for men, women, and children, the latest in audio-video and home electronics, some of the world's most popular perfumes, colognes, and beauty supplies, jewelry — from 14k gold and diamonds to costume reproductions. In addition there are: plants, handbags (designer), furniture, records and tapes, footwear, dancewear, sportswear and goods, and kitchenware. You'll even find a variety of home improvement services, tools, insurance and financial services. Just looking at one of the items lists boggles the mind. They seem to have more of a variety than even some of the major retail department stores. Some of their brand names rival that of the shops found on Rodeo Drive, a popular shopping mecca for quality designer goods.

The record vendor

At just one of the meets there are over six hundred vendors, while the other location houses three hundred. Each exhibitor is allowed to design and build his own display using whatever creativity he deems necessary to attract shoppers to his area. The only thing that it could be compared to is the appearance of a trade show, in which vendors are sectioned off, usually reposing side by side, in order to form a long continuous aisle. In this way shoppers have only

The crowds

to stroll the length of one aisle, glancing from side to side to take in all of the merchandise.

Since each vendor sells individually, the shopper deals with him directly at the booth, so there are no checkout lines to delay the hurried patron. The vendors work to sell as much of their inventory as possible in the three days each week that the swap meet is open. In the case of these two California locations, their sale days were listed as Friday, Saturday, and Sunday. The hours were between 10:00 A.M. and 8:00 P.M. The vendors seemed to all agree on one point when I asked them what their strategy was. Apparently, the name of the game is to sell out before the end of the weekend. The only thing that seems to be a little unsettling is that the prices may fluctuate daily, sometimes hourly as the competition among the vendors begins to take on a heated atmosphere. The selection of goods is usually better in the early morning, but the prices are often better later in the afternoon as the vendors try to get rid of their remaining merchandise. These last desperate moments are the reason a shopper can suddenly hear a chorus of chants and enticements coming from the vendors, who will do anything to attract your last minute attention in the closing hours.

Prices are the main reason why thousands of people are flocking to these weekend events. One vendor who specialized in designer clothing for women said that she was able to pick up a line of summer jackets from a major designer. She had bought four dozen and sold out in one weekend, listing the jackets at twenty-nine dollars each. At that time, they were selling at Saks and Robinsons for seventy-five dollars. It is not unusual to find an Arthur Max dress for ninety dollars at one of these indoor meets, when Bloomingdale's wants three hundred and fifty dollars for the same product.

The stereo man

There are literally hundreds of merchants under one roof. Each booth is built, owned, and operated by the merchant. These are not people who just throw down a blanket and lay out their wares. They are professional business people from within the community who are there on a permanent basis. There are hundreds of representatives from the major garment district offering the latest in fashions. There are dozens of representatives from the jewelry mart. There are furniture distributors, bakeries, home and garden nurseries, importers, wholesalers, beauty supply distributors, and hundreds of others representing virtually every consumer goods group.

The indoor booth

Some of the designer fashion labels include: Jimmy Z, Cherokee, and I.D. In beauty supplies there are: Jhirmack, Nexus Infusium, and Paul Mitchell. In electronics, such names can be found: Sony, Fisher, Hitachi, and Panasonic. They carry brand name footwear: Reebok, Nike, L.A. Gear, and Puma to name a few. Everything from disk players to toys, the indoor swap meets seem to have it all. This is certainly convenient for the shopper. Even the admission price of one dollar is digestible. At one location there was free parking for up to one thousand five hundred cars. Senior citizens and children free? You bet! Really, you can't go wrong from the shopping end of it. But what about the seller who wishes to set up and display? There are a few rules and regulations but the potential seller couldn't have it any better if it came to him on a silver platter.

The lamp lady

THE INDOOR SELLER

How difficult is it to set up and become a merchant at an indoor swap meet facility? Not terribly. There are some prerequisites and guidelines that you will be required to follow. One of the first and foremost is a valid Resale Permit from the State Board of Equalization. You can obtain this by finding a State Board of Equalization Office list and getting in touch with your local business tax field office, paying a fee, and filling out the necessary forms. Do this first. Without the permit you won't be able to sell anything.

The next thing that you will want to do is to visit your local indoor meet (if you are fortunate enough to have one in your vicinity). If there is no space available you will have to fill out a waiting list. The fact that you will have to wait is very likely since these meets are becoming more popular. On the waiting list application you will fill out your name, business name if you have one, address, phone number, business phone number, the type of merchandise that you have for sale, the number of booth spaces that you want along with their type and location, and a little history regarding your previous swap meet sales experience. They also might want to know if you can be ready to maintain your booth on an off-day schedule, i.e., during Christmastime or some other special occasion.

By filling out the waiting list application and turning it in, you will automatically be considered when there is an opening in the swap meet. In the case of the Valley Indoor Swap Meet, their rule says that space only becomes available once every four weeks, and they use the waiting list to select prospective vendors. So there is a minor screening period in which the management can look over a waiting list application to determine if you are going to present a good prospect to the meet or not. All spaces are sold on a four week block basis. After each block, those spaces that are not renewed are offered to prospective vendors from the waiting list. They select vendors who they feel are best suited to fill the vacancy. As soon as a space is available, they contact the new vendor and allow him to move in.

If you have passed the first test of initiation and have been assigned a booth area, you will be required to fill out a contract or license agreement. At some indoor swap meets the management buys a blanket permit and issues each individual his own permit. We will examine a license agreement that is of this variety.

On the license agreement you will be asked to fill out your company name, business phone, form of ownership, DBA, P/S or corporation, your address, resale permit number, and the type of merchandise that you intend to sell. You will be asked if you need electricity or not — this is important if you are selling radios or televisions and other electrically operated merchandise.

Included in the agreement will be a clause like the following example:

"I hereby apply for a Seller's Permit which would enable me to sell at the Swap Meet. I understand that the issuing of said Seller's Permit constitutes an agreement between myself as Vendor and the Management of the Swap Meet. I further agree to comply with all Rules and Regulations and understand that the Swap Meet management reserves the exclusive right to designate any and all selling spaces that I am licensed to sell from. I understand that my licensing privileges may be revoked for rules violations."

This clause is pretty standard in that it is asking the vendor if he is willing to comply with the judgment of the management. The management is reserving the right to select a booth for you, in the event that they cannot find your exact requirement. For instance, if you originally wanted a 20 foot by 20 foot garden booth in the northwest corner, and the booth was not available, you would be obliged to take a similar location if the management deemed it necessary. Of course, you could decline the location, but then you would have to wait for the specific location that you requested. The last sentence in the clause means that you are subject to the rules that appear in the license agreement, and any other authority that the management wishes to dictate.

Another clause goes on to state:

"Vendor is a licensee only. This agreement is not intended to create a landlord-tenant relationship. Term of this license is for the dates indicated on your receipt and may be renewed automatically for each succeeding period of time that vendor space is sold by the mutual consent of both the vendor and the Swap Meet management. All merchandise and other property must be removed from the space at the end of the term. Vendor shall remain open for business at all times that the Swap Meet is open for business. Vendor shall conduct only the retail type of business that he/she is licensed for only from the space assigned by Management. Booth construction (i.e., walls and flooring) become a permanent fixture within the swap meet and may not be removed or demolished by licensee upon termination of license."

The first three sentences of this clause actually redefine an important fact — that is, the vendor is on a semi-permanent basis and must renew at the prescribed times, in this case every four weeks. If the vendor does not wish to renew his license he must vacate the booth removing all of his merchandise. The vendor is required to be open when the swap meet is open and this could include extra days that are prescribed by the management. Absenteeism is not allowed. The last sentence in this clause states that anything that you build to accommodate your merchandise: walls, flooring, shelves, dividers, etc. will become the permanent property of the swap meet when you leave. This would mean anchored fixtures and not display cases, racks, and portable display fixtures.

A third clause goes on to say:

"Only the merchandise specified above may be sold from the designated space. All merchandise must be displayed within the boundaries of the designated space and may not extend out into the aisles that are public walkways. The following articles may not be sold:

A. Guns, ammunition, fireworks, or explosives of any kind.
B. Illegal items, pornographic materials or anything which in the sole opinion of Management is objectionable.
C. Food, drink, or other edible items without the express written approval of Management.
D. Alcoholic beverages.
E. Live pets of any kind without written approval from the County Health Department."

This third clause is standard and self-explanatory. We will continue on with the rest of the agreement and number the rest of the clauses, and add comment after them if needed:

4) Vendor shall not sell, transfer, assign or sublease space or permit anyone else to occupy it or conduct business from the space.

5) Vendors and their employees are admitted through the designated Vendor entrances only. Vendors and their employees are required to park their vehicles in the designated vendor parking areas. Employees of the Vendors arriving after 10:00 A.M. must have an employee pass or they will be required to pay the regular entrance fee. Vendors must have their permits available for inspection in order to gain entrance to the building. No entrance will be allowed except during authorized times.

6) All business conducted by the Vendor or his employees must be performed so as not to infringe upon the rights of other sellers or in any manner offend the public attending the event. Should the Vendor wish to hand out samples or written material, this must take place from within the Vendor's designated space(s).

Clause number six means that the management does not want the Vendor wandering up and down the aisles soliciting personal business. You are confined to your area — you must stay there to conduct business.

7) Vendor assumes sole risk of loss, theft, or damage to merchandise and other personal property belonging to vendor while such property or merchandise is in or on the swap meet premises. Vendor acknowledges that management assumes no responsibility to insure the safety or to protect the property of the Vendor from fire, rain, theft, malicious mischief, accident, or any other cause beyond the providing of security officers and/or security systems.

Number seven states emphatically that you are on your own. Management is not responsible for your misfortunes, whether they are a minor accident or major catastrophe.

8) No refunds will be made of any payments made under this license for any reason. Management reserves the right to terminate this license agreement for any violation of these rules and regulations. In the event of such termination, the Vendor is not entitled to receive any portion of any payments made under this license.

9) Management reserves the right to cancel this agreement prior to the commencement of the term on three days written notice. Said notice will be deemed given on deposit in the mail or on personal delivery, whichever is first. On such cancellation Vendor shall receive a refund of money paid.

This means that if after you have been accepted as a vendor, the management decides that they have made a mistake in selecting you, they are within their rights to terminate the agreement. But they must do so in the time specified and give you a refund.

10) All booth materials and other property used in the conduct of business from the space must be approved in accordance with local governmental codes. No booth may be taller than eight feet or be constructed in a manner that might constitute an obstruction or hazard to the public. Building and Safety and Fire Department codes and regulations must be adhered to at all times, including the following:

A. All extension cords must have grounded outlets or be polarized.
B. All fabrics used for securing your booth or used for display must be fire retardant and display a fire retardant label.

11) Renewals are to be paid in full, no later than 6:00 P.M. on the third Sunday of each week block. NOTE: this is one full week prior to the actual expiration of each four week block period.

12) A fifteen dollar fee will be imposed for every returned check and vendor's space reservation will be canceled.

This clause could present a problem as it could tie in with clause number thirteen. In the event that you give the licensor a bad check, they state that they will, not "can," cancel your reservation. If you are set up at the time and they do decide to terminate your agreement, you could possibly be charged the one hundred fifty dollar penalty for merchandise left behind if you did not remove it in time upon their order. It is doubtful that management would follow through with such a severe penalty action, but if the situation was a nasty disagreement or fight, it is possible that they would exercise this maximum option.

13) Vendors will be charged one hundred fifty dollars storage fee for merchandise left in or on the space or swap meet premises after expiration of term plus a removal charge.

14) Vendors are to open their booth during all times the swap meet is open. No push carts or dollies are to be in the aisles once the swap meet is open for business as it constitutes a safety hazard to the public.

15) Refusal to bring your booth up to fire codes or building and safety codes once instructed to do so will result in immediate termination of your seller's permit.

This means that the licensor is directly responsible to the city for any violations that you commit. This is because you are under the blanket authority of the licensor. If you commit a code violation your licensor is warned, fined, or both.

16) Any and all prior negotiations are superseded by this license agreement. No terms relating to this agreement may be changed or added unless in writing and signed by the licensor.

This means that any negotiations or agreements, verbal or otherwise, that went on before you signed the contract, don't count. If you thought that you had made a deal for a choice booth, because the management told you so beforehand, unless it is in writing in the present contract it is not recognized. Only the current agreement and what it states within it are valid.

17) The issuing by Management of a Seller's Permit to a Vendor constitutes an agreement by that Vendor to comply with all rules and regulations. In the event that a Vendor fails to comply with the Rules and Regulations, Management retains the right to restrict, exclude, or evict the Vendor. Management assumes no responsibility for any items lost, stolen, or damaged, regardless of the cause. Vendor agrees to hold management harmless from any liability or damage arising from the Vendor's use of the premises and/or injury to persons or property resulting from items sold or exchanged by Vendor thereon. Vendor assumes full responsibility for all merchandise the Vendor offers for sale. Legal proceedings, if any, will also include attorney's fees and court costs to the prevailing party.

This last clause is pretty much a summary that says you are to follow and obey all of the previous rules and regulations. The last portion of the clause is telling you that you are really on your own and responsible for everything that is associated with your business. Lawsuits, and accidents that require hospitalization, or court costs incurred through injury are strictly the responsibility of the vendor, and in no way can the licensor be held liable for any damages or misfortunes.

Let's take a look at some of the common questions that the prospective seller might ask about indoor swap meets:

Q. Do I need any licenses in order to sell at the Indoor Swap Meet?
A. You are only required to have a valid Resale Permit. No city licenses are necessary as we collect a City Tax of $1.50 per day.

Q. Am I restricted from selling certain types of merchandise?
A. Yes. No food items of any kind, no guns, no pornography or anything illegal may be sold.

Q. Can I store my merchandise on the premises throughout the week?
A. Yes. There is no extra charge for weekly storage in your booth. We have a limited amount of additional storage space that is rented out for a nominal fee when available.

Q. What about loading, unloading, and booth construction. When will I be able to do this?
A. All of that information will be given to you when you receive your Seller's Permit.

Q. If I take a booth now, can I later transfer to a different booth site if one becomes available?
A. Yes. We generally try and accommodate the requests of our existing sellers before offering the space to those on our waiting list.

Q. Is it advisable to show samples of my merchandise to people in the business office?
A. Yes. The more information we have on you, the better the chances you have on filling the vacant spaces when they become available.

Q. What are the benefits of having an indoor Swap Meet?
A. No rainouts. No wind blowing over your display or damaging your merchandise, which means that the public will attend regardless of the weather conditions. No early morning set up and late day tear down. You can leave your merchandise for the entire week if you wish. You can build a permanent display which will afford you more repeat business as you develop your own clientele.

Q. Are utilities available?
A. Yes. You may install your own telephone at your booth site. Electricity is available for the cost of installation plus a nominal monthly fee.

Q. What is the length of the licensing agreement?
A. All spaces are sold on a four week block basis. At the end of the four week period you will be given first option to renew your booth location.

Q. Can I improve my booth site?
A. Yes. In fact we encourage it. Any style or design is fine as long as it conforms to the fire codes.

Q. Can you tell me a little bit about the costs of renting a booth site? How much and what are the sizes?
A. Spaces are sold in blocks of four weekends (twelve selling dates) only. You are welcome to store your merchandise on the premises for the entire block if you want. Storage charges are included in the four week block rates. Regular booths (twelve days) are $320. Outside corner booths (twelve days) are $360. Main aisle booths (twelve days) are $425. Garden areas (twelve days) are $250. At this location all booth areas measure 10 feet by 10 feet except for the garden areas, which are 8 feet by 10 feet.

In lieu of an Annual Gross Receipts Tax, there is a City Tax of $18 per block ($1.50 per selling date). We are authorized to collect this sum at the time of your rental. Electricity can be supplied to any booth through our licensed contractor at a normal charge. The monthly charge for electricity is $25 per four week block.

Admission booth

We only accept cash, cashier's checks, or money orders; we will not accept personal checks.

In summary I will say that the indoor swap meet concept looks like a pretty good bet all around for the shopper, and for the person who wishes to begin a small business for the first time. The concept negates the high overhead costs of owning or renting larger store property when the monthly amounts can reach into the thousands of dollars. Not to mention Triple Net costs, high city taxes, and other expenditures. It is a chance to own and operate a mini-shop that is incorporated into the facility of a large network. There would certainly be no need to feel lonely with so many other vendors in close proximity. All said, the Indoor Swap Meet concept is a bright idea and a chance for the little guy to enter into the realm of mass market retail without losing his shirt in the process.

Note: Excerpts, clauses, and questions and answers were taken from actual license agreements and documents from Metropolitan Marketing, Inc., sponsor of the Valley Indoor Swap Meet in California. Licenses, permit requirements, rules and regulations, and fees may vary with other indoor marketing systems. These are examples from actual working Indoor Swap Meets.

Chapter Thirteen

THE DAY IS DONE

Back to Mother's House

Most swap meets and garage sales begin to wind down at around 3:00 P.M. The larger swap meets close at 4:00 P.M. or 5:00 P.M. This is because business traffic starts to slacken; people want to beat the crowds home, and supper is not too far off. If you are still busy during this time there is no reason why you can't continue with your sale until you are satisfied that you have served the very last customer. If business is down to a mere trickle, you might want to begin packing up leftover merchandise. Or perhaps one last spark in the sale is called for.

COUNT YOUR CABBAGE AND SMILE

If you have done everything right in your sale, you will have cabbage to count. Money. This was, after all, the primary reason for the sale: to make a profit. The learning experience and new friendships are certainly important, but a garage sale that is a financial success is the best motivation for you to try another one. There are a few more things you can do to squeeze out some additional profit just before the end of the sale.

When things are slowing down you can adjust your prices to make a few last ditch sales. You might re-tag your items with your lower asking price. Or you could verbally announce the lower price change to interested customers, telling them that you are willing to take a reduction. In the last minutes of the sale, you might put a "best offer" sign on each of your tables and take bids; this would help sharpen your bartering skills. Then, if an offer sounds reasonable, and you don't foresee any loss, you can accept.

Strangely enough, the end of a sale is a good time for someone to make a bid out. Granted, the selection will be sparse, the quality goods fewer, but it is still an opportunity for a seller to end a sale with a bang instead of a whimper. To end a sale with a bid out, your sale price will have to be low. The lower it is, the more irresistible it becomes for the customer. You can also sell just tables of items in a block or group. Maybe you will let table one go for $25.00, table two for $17.50, and table three for $35.00. Undoubtedly, you will find yourself playing auctioneer with this set up, taking the highest bid per table. Experiment. Ask the customers for their opinion. It can't hurt in the last minutes of the sale. But for Pete's sake, don't get carried away and sell the tables!

All told, when the day of the sale is over, if you have made less than $50.00 you have done something wrong. This applies even to a small sale. Personally, and depending upon my inventory, if I have made less than $300.00, I've done something very wrong. Fortunately, this does not happen very often. The $300.00 that I am referring to is the profit amount after my investments. This is my net profit. My average take is around $300.00 to $400.00 for a two day weekend sale. I have hit higher marks of over a $1,000.00 but these have been few and extraordinary cases. Over $1,000.00 is not unusual if I have "buddy sold." Meaning that I have had a neighbor or friend who was an equal contributor to the sale. Of course, profits are divided up according to what was sold and who it belonged to. A buddy sale (relatives are good prospects) helps to puff up the size of the sale by adding more merchandise, hence, a bigger selection. A larger sale draws more interest.

If you make an inventory list and keep track of your sales, compare your total cash take against the amount that you have tallied on your list. If there are any mistakes, it usually means that you made an error in counting change back, or you took a reduced bid on something and forgot about it. Major errors might indicate that you actually forgot to collect on a purchase; this happens when you find yourself busy with more than one customer at a time. It's always best to follow through with each individual sale from beginning to end. This avoids confusion.

BREAKING CAMP

When your sale is over, it is over. There is no sense in prolonging it into the night, dragging out the floodlights, and such. Instead, consider packing up your unsold goods and placing them back into your storage place: in the case of a swap meet, your truck or van; in the garage sale, your garage or storage facility. Just remember to keep your consignment items separate from your belongings, ready for transport back to their owners. Organize and pack neatly; there is always the possibility of another sale, with the addition of some fresh items.

After clearing your driveway or booth area, transport your consignment items back to their original owners as soon as you can. The sooner the better.

Such things are easily forgotten or put off until another time. When delivering the consignment items, the time to pay the owners is then and there, promptly and in full. There is no reason to pay your consignment people with anything other than cash. If you have made numerous consignment sales, you will certainly have the money to pay them. No excuses. Don't forget to thank them for their participation. If you have plans for future sales, mention this to them, and see if they are agreeable to another try. In case you have failed to sell consignment goods, explain your regrets to the owners and assure them that the next time might be better.

Your next item of business will be to remember if you have made any arrangements for follow-up visits or calls. It is possible that during your sale you told a customer that you would call them and find out if they were pleased with a purchase. Or there might have been a question as to the operability of an item, in which the customer had to take the item home to see if it worked or fit into his system. You might want to follow up personally, and help a customer with a setup or connection procedure. It could be as trivial as hooking up an aquarium equipped with a pump and filter, or as complicated as the installation and operation of a multi-component stereo system. The important point in follow-up service is to assure customer satisfaction, because the time to confront a problem is immediately, when memories and facts are fresh in the mind. You would be surprised at how appreciative people are when given this slight amenity. It saves you headaches in the long run, and such courtesies are not forgotten.

Your last order of business will be to retrieve all of your signs, banners, and flyers. Don't leave them out overnight. The moisture could loosen the tape and your advertisements could end up on the sidewalks and streets, come morning. A little wind, and before you know it, they're flapping down the street, this time with a new purpose — litter. Take them down at the end of your sale and store them away for future use — you can always use the backsides. Then you can rest easy in the knowledge that some community member won't come hammering on your door, wanting to know why your personal advertisements are all over the public byways.

It's finally over. You're probably tired and wondering where all the hours went. You might even be a little sad too, because it was fun, wasn't it? It was actually exciting meeting new neighbors, maybe for the first time. You've probably never talked so much in your life, or so it seems. You were on stage for a while. Your acting abilities, charm, and salesmanship were really put to the test. You feel that you have never had so much direct attention from the public in so short a time period. There's a good chance that you have discovered that people really like you — your personality, your opinions, your ideas. You even met what's her face, two houses down, and she's coming over for coffee next Tuesday. Strange, but you never knew that she belonged to the Romance Writers of America. Of course, you never asked her. Then there's Bill, that wonderful old man who promised to take you to the park and show you how model airplanes are really supposed to fly. And then there's Linda from across the street, the lady who told you that she could give your toy poodle that extra special cut, for a song and a dance. And so it goes.

Your back hurts a little, but it's a good feeling. Gosh, you feel like you've worked all week without a break. You forgot all about sweeping the driveway, because right now you're just a little too tired to do any more. You'll do that in the morning. And hey! You have half of the rent money! That means that you have a little extra — maybe that video recorder on sale? Or it could be that...Gee, congratulations are in order. You decide to give yourself that pat on your sore back.

As you shuffle into your house and collapse on the sofa, you're struck by a certain thought, "Well, what's next?" Then you decide that you don't have to think about future campaigns just now. All that's left is to relax. So you sit back and put your feet up. Then you count your cabbage...and smile.

AFTERWORD

The origin of the garage or yard sale is shrouded in mystery. It's because no one has ever gone to great lengths to discover its past — it simply isn't the topic of the day, nor will it ever be, I imagine. An unreliable source has traced it back to 1895, where Clara Ford, while her husband's back was turned, decided to pitch all of his tools and mechanical knickknacks out onto the lawn where those who passed were assailed by a brightly painted sign that read: "No reasonable offer refused."

Since the husband of Clara Ford was none other than Henry Ford, of Ford Motor Company fame, we are quite pleased to hear after all of these years that the lawn sale was a dismal failure. And this was due, according to rumor, to the lack of proper advertisement. If Clara had succeeded, we might all be engaged in a more reliable and efficient means of transportation: the horse and buggy. But we do have Clara to thank for her feminine intuition. She, as well as her husband, was truly the start of "something big." Perhaps she realized the practicality and necessity of her venture: to offer something to the public that was meaningless to her, but still held some measure of value to one who was in need. It was a gamble to be sure, but one that she was not afraid to take, since the risks were so minimal and the rewards so great. By way of her own expression she has shown us that the general public can be pleased in ways other than that of dreams of gigantic corporations and assembly lines.

Maybe it was her way of protesting the emergence of the "corporation giganticus." For whatever the reason, we owe her a debt of thanks. Because everything that has happened since then, in the way of yard and garage sales, has taught us a lesson in business ethics: that the little person can truly make a difference when all of the other little people are at his side with the same intention. This leads us to some present day thought.

Everyone knows that if the nation was to shop garage, swap meet, and auction sales exclusively, our economy would collapse. Without private business and the major industrial corporations to recirculate our money, we would find ourselves in an "open loop" economy. Trade would suffer as a result. We need trading on a major scale to survive. We must supply the needs of others while we in turn procure what we need from others to survive. Therefore, it is recommended that the average consumer look upon garage and swap meet sales as an alternative in shopping. They are not intended to serve as a sole means of regular trading. They do not hold the solution to the whole of consumerism.

Virtually none of our products are recycled. We live by the adage, "out with the old, in with the new." It is a familiar credo. Our society creates, uses, and discards as a normal function in our economy. Sometimes our disposal habits and wasteful actions are premature. This is because it is "chic" or "now" to have the latest products on the market. Is it any wonder that it is so easy to overextend ourselves with credit? It has become too convenient to buy things. We can take immediate possession of products in exchange for promises to pay. We end up paying more for products through interest rates because we utilize the privilege.

Garage sales, swap meets, and auctions are big business. Violette McKevitt, a well known professional in the field of estate sales, has said that literally billions of dollars of items have been thrown away, according to a source she read. We can safely assume that billions of dollars have been made in these sideline businesses. Where has the dignity of the common garage sale evaporated? Have we always been just a little bit ashamed of it? It certainly warrants our financial attention. It's probably been the proving ground for some of the most successful salespersons in the nation. I'm always wondering if it doesn't deserve a more rightful place in our heritage and culture. Its roots might have begun with the first caveman who offered up some used bones in trade for some shiny rocks.

Wherever it came from, I'm sure glad that it's here. I'm not ashamed to say that I am proud of it. I've never been a salesman, nor will I ever be one, but it's given me a chance to experience new friends. It's paid my rent more than once. And it has given me a sense of accomplishment and worth. I don't think that I will ever stop. I hope that you don't either. It's just my way of saying, "Come one, come all," I hope you have a good time finding whatever your heart desires.

ACTION LIST FOR BUYER

☐ Make sure that you have precise directions on how to get to your garage or swap meet sale. Have a passenger assist you.

☐ Are dressed casually? Simple street clothes are sufficient when visiting garage sales and swap meets. Don't give anyone the impression that "money" is your middle name.

☐ Avoid driving your most expensive vehicle to garage sales. If you can't help it, park the Mercedes some distance down the street from the sale.

☐ If en route to an antique auction, do you have pencil and pad for notes? A guidebook to identify and record prices of antiques?

☐ If you are interested in motorized toys or appliances, have you remembered to bring an extra extension cord and different sized (fresh) batteries?

☐ Do you have cash on hand?

☐ Will you ask before you handle merchandise?

☐ Will you ask for demonstrations of hardware and appliances? You are entitled, you know.

☐ If you put a deposit down at a moving sale, are you going to make sure that you return in time to pick up your purchase or the deposit?

☐ Do you plan on getting to the sale as soon as possible? In the case of an auction, are you going to the pre-sale to examine the inventory? Are you taking a tape measure along so that you can measure large pieces?

☐ Is your vehicle large enough to accommodate pieces of furniture if you plan to buy them?

☐ Do you have some rope, bungy cord, tape, blankets, or pads to help you tie down merchandise? How about some cardboard boxes and newspapers for the transport of fragile items?

☐ If you are buying a brand name component are you receiving a guarantee or warranty with it?

□ Be extremely careful when considering pets for sale. Pets can carry parasites, germs, bacteria, and some infectious diseases. Refrain from buying pets if you can, except from classified private party ads.

□ Don't purchase questionable merchandise that does not have I.D. labels or serial numbers — the goods might be stolen.

□ Don't buy food products at common garage sales. There are City Health Codes against selling such products by private party without the proper permits.

□ Speed limits in housing tracts are usually twenty-five miles per hour. In school zones the limit is as low as fifteen miles per hour. Drive safely — be observant of children.

□ Do you have a precise idea of what you are looking for? Is it a specialty item that can be found in the classifieds? A few phone calls wouldn't hurt before you go on your search.

□ Are you going to ask if a seller has a return or money back guarantee? It is uncommon with used merchandise, but it will not hurt to ask.

□ Will you be patient with other family members and realize that they have their interests in a sale too? Give other family members equal time with their shopping desires.

ACTION LIST FOR SELLER

(See also Seller Responsibility list in Chapter 10)

□ Have you gathered and organized items together that you plan to sell?

□ Are your mechanical and electrical items functional?

□ Is your merchandise clean and ready for presentation — electrical outlets available, light bulbs, batteries?

□ Are your display tables ready? If not, do you know that you can make them with regular household items?

□ Are there any people, friends, relatives and neighbors who would like to donate items to your sale?

□ Do you have a good mixture of male/female items?

□ Are you sure that you are not selling items that do not belong to you? If you are, do you have permission?

□ Are you using all of your advertising routes to bring your sale to the attention of the public? How about flyers, banners, and signs? Newspaper advertisement? Ads in the shopping magazines? Are your ads timed to coincide with your sale?

□ Do you want to visit other sales and try a "bid out" to help stock your own sale?

□ Are you going to arrange your tables and display platforms for maximum viewing?

□ Will you make sure that your driveway and curb area are cleared of your own vehicles to allow the public convenient access?

□ Will you make an inventory list of your sale items?

□ Will you tag sale items or encourage verbal offers?

□ Are you prepared to deal with problem items? Some minor repairs? Will you be offering some type of guarantee or tradeback policy? Do you plan to do any follow-up service for customers to insure satisfaction?

□ Are you prepared to pay taxes on profits if they are substantial?

□ If you are interested in becoming an indoor or outdoor swap meet vendor, are you ready to follow the guidelines of the management? Will you pay the proper fees for booth space and permits?

□ Are you aware that there are city ordinances that forbid a resident to hold more than ten garage sales in a calendar year? You should check with your city to find out if such limitations exist.

□ Will you be sure to keep all of your sale merchandise displayed on your property? It is against the law to place articles on the sidewalk and street because they constitute a hazard — they are public byways.

□ Are you going to end your sale at a reasonable hour and not persist into the night, which could irritate your neighbors?

□ When it is all over, and you've struck down all signs of your sale, will you count your cabbage and smile?

BIBLIOGRAPHY

Boger, Louise. *House and Garden's Antiques.* New York, Simon & Schuster, 1973.

Phelp, Peter et al., *Antiques.* Great Britain, Octopus Books, 1973.

Johnson, Bruce. *$20,000 A Year in Antiques and Collectibles.* New York, Rawson Associates, 1986.

Margolius, Sidney. *The Consumer's Guide to Better Buying.* New York, Pocket Books, 1974.

Graf, Rudolf. *Radio Shack Dictionary of Electronics.* Indianapolis, Howard W. Sams and Co., Inc., 1972.

INDEX